MW00694905

THE PSYCHIC SOVIET

THE PSYCHIC SOVIET

I. F. Svenonius

THE
PSYCHIC
SOVIET

AND OTHER WORKS BY
Ian F. Svenonius

EXPANDED EDITION

BROOKLYN, NEW YORK, USA
BALLYDEHOB, CO. CORK, IRELAND

Published by Akashic Books
© 2006, 2020 Ian F. Svenonius

Originally published in an earlier form in 2006 by Drag City Inc., Chicago, IL. Proofreading by David Grubbs. Illustrations by I.F. Svenonius. Photography by Garnett Soles. Production by Scott McGaughey. Layout by Dan Osborn.

Versions of some of these essays were originally published elsewhere, such as in the periodicals *Index, BB Gun, Sound Collector, Audio Review, Dot Dot Dot, Plan B, Portland Mercury, Weird War World*, among others. Thanks to those who encouraged and published them, particularly Jesse Pearson, and *Index* and *BB Gun* magazines.

ISBN-13: 978-1-61775-766-2
Library of Congress Control Number: 2019935268
All rights reserved
First Akashic Books printing
Printed in China

Akashic Books
Brooklyn, New York, USA
Ballydehob, Co. Cork, Ireland
Twitter: @AkashicBooks
Facebook: AkashicBooks
E-mail: info@akashicbooks.com
Website: www.akashicbooks.com

Dedicated to M-26-7

CONTENTS

INSTRUCTIONS

This volume should clear up much of the confusion regarding events of the last millennium—artistic, geopolitical, philosophical, et al.

Its small size will make it easy to carry around so as to refer to in case of ethical quandaries, arguments, and social feuds. It is intended for such "street" use, hence the durable sleeve and paper stock.

Feel free to scribble rebuttals and notations in the generous margins of the book itself. Or to quote it aloud. This is intended as a *living volume*.

None of this collection is to be confused with so-called academia. Instead, it is a kind of free verse, outside of science or respectability and at liberty to flaunt its diabolical exhumations on its user.

The reader is invited to participate in the

use of the book not only by scanning it with his or her eyes, but also by running a finger up and down its spine. It should be passed around when it is finished so as to proliferate its explanations, theories, and inventions.

The Psychic Soviet may not be used in certain situations, or by certain people, or on certain occasions. Such conditions should be self-evident, and we trust that its user shall act responsibly and appropriately if such a circumstance or situation should arise.

I.F.S.

CENTRAL COMMITTEE
RRC

THE PSYCHIC SOVIET

THE PSYCHIC SOVIET

The Cold War in Psycho-Geopolitics

> *The first class opposition that appears in history coincides with the development of the antagonism between man and woman in monogamous marriage, and the first class oppression coincides with that of the female sex by the male.*

FRIEDRICH ENGELS

I. PSD

The collapse of the Soviet Union was the most grievous psychological event in recent history.

Though referred to officially in bourgeois society as moral fable and totem of God's will, this calamity—the 1991 defeat of international socialism—has plunged the population of the world into a state of nihilism and despair.

Though this depression is recognized

as a global crisis, its cause is not widely ac-
knowledged or even understood. Even so,
the post-Soviet world is a place haunted by
its former inhabitant and the nature of that
inhabitant's demise. The fantastic popularity
of antidepressants is just one symptom of a
"Post-Soviet Depression" (PSD) syndrome.
Other signs of PSD are worse and more
far-reaching in re: to their long-term effects.

The idealism that once characterized
Homo sapiens, for example, seems to have vanished. Instead of drawing up hopeful plans for
the future, or engaging his signature feature—
ingenuity—he now stares vacantly into the
abyss. Meanwhile, the earth is steered toward
apocalypse by its most deranged element.

Man's new fatalism reveals that he, like his
leaders, has become deranged. Once he was a
crusader for this or for that. Now, in the throes
of PSD, he is either an idiot, a "kook," or just
a transcendental lecher. He holds the future in
open contempt. His brain is just a warehouse
for putrefied cynicism. His only appetite is for
sensory and sensual "kicks"; garden-variety

vulgarities devised to keep him numb and perpetuate idiocy.

For him, the end of the Cold War signaled, instead of a chance to proliferate peace and equality, an accelerated reiteration of the Neroism and barbarity that had characterized his most abject moments. It marked the final, hopeless capitulation to Abaddon.

The "war on terror" and its various offspring (renditions, invasions, space weapons, torture chambers, et al.) are just the grotesque ejaculations of the USSR's malfunctioning, off-balance—albeit victorious—archnemesis, the USA. They were inevitable after and foretold by the far grander, much misrepresented, and strangely underplayed superevent known as "The Socialist Collapse."

Why, though, should the undoing of an institution so universally despised and as disfigured by revisionist historical framing as Soviet socialism precipitate such cosmic depression? The USSR was—and still is—everyone's favorite punching bag.

The answer, though not altogether rational, reveals an unconscious understanding of events barred from the official narrative of history.

II. PSYCHO-GEO-TICS

Politically delineated "state" entities, although they are contrived abstractions, nonetheless have deep and resonant associations for what psychologist Carl Jung referred to as the collective unconscious, or "mass mind." These geopolitical characters are a constellation referred to as much as the family in the self's determination of identity, their fortunes often determined by their inhabitants blind, convulsive will.

Political constructs such as national/racial identity or the emotional attachment to a state's leader are sublimated projection: the cloying gurgles of an infant child. They make no sense even to their mewing dispatchers.

They are simply the voiced rationalizations for a deeply rooted identification with (or, perhaps, alienation from) nation-states (not only one's own, but all perceived states) as archetypes in a system of astral-political deities.

This phenomenon, whereby the politically contrived abstraction of the nation assumes an archetypal character or persona, is an intrinsic quality to mankind and is called "psychological geopolitics," or "psycho-geo-tics" for short.

Psycho-geo-tic conflict is perhaps best exemplified by one of its many ancient examples—the warrior city-state Sparta versus democratic Athens—but has been an underlying current in human history long before that particular S&M duo was conjured up by Greek perverts. Lord Byron was acting out a psycho-geo-tic impulse centuries later when he joined the Greek war against the Turks and jumped to his death in the Bosporus. (Byron, being a Romantic-era "animal man," was more prone than normal people to act on psycho-geo-tic instinct.) The confrontation between Vietnam and the United States—a more recent event—is shrouded in much psycho-geo-tic "fuzz"; US motorcycle enthusiasts still wistfully yearn for that war, which gave full expression to barbaric impulses repressed at home by the civil rights movement. Though transnational conflicts all have their materialist/political root causes (e.g., imperialism), the manipulation of primitive psychology ("psy-ops") is key to rallying support for mass violence.

In the modern era, especially since World War II but even before that, no players in psychological geopolitics have been as emotionally significant as the USA and the USSR. In a Jungian sense, these two constructs represent a maternal/paternal dialectic, with the military alliances they spawned, the "Warsaw Pact" and "NATO," representing competing familial clans.

The USA was the father and the USSR, dominated by "Mother Russia," was of course the mother. The Cold War was, to the primitive psyche of the spectator, a parental schism of cosmic proportion, with the inhabitants of the earth caught in the ensuing megastruggle for the children's loyalty.

That divorce rates exploded through the tenure of the Cold War was a direct result of this latent gender identification and the chronic ill-defined state of war which existed between the two sexual proxies: a situation which mirrored a fractious, warring household.

III. MOTHER

On the one hand was the socialist East. Though popularly ridiculed as an evil "slave state," the USSR's politburo was acutely concerned with feminism right from its inception. Socialist philosophers Marx, Engels, Fourier, Kollontai, and Bebel all addressed sexual inequality in their tracts and had come to the conclusion that "There can be no emancipation of humanity without the social independence and equality of the sexes" (Bebel, 1879).

Alexandra Kollontai described the family as a "microscopic state where husband ruled wife and children" that must be replaced with a type of "free union, fortified by the love and mutual respect of the two members of the Workers' State, equal in their rights and in their obligations." Since Marxists thought subordinate and dominant relationships had as their root cause capitalist property relationships, they naturally assumed the abolition of this root cause would engender equality between the sexes. According to Engels, it was the accumulation of surplus value through capitalist production that had allowed men to dominate and exploit women—who were bound to the house, and therefore had no salable labor value (because of the devaluation that capitalism places on housework)—so the introduction of women into the workforce, along with the abolition of property, would solve gender inequality, which permeated all societies.

The Soviet Union's constitution therefore proclaimed women's equality with men in all spheres of life, and the 1918 Soviet Family Code established the right of free choice in marriage, division of housework, abortion rights, women's property rights, et al. Housework was to be a collective assignment, along with raising children. Lenin decried the housewife as a "domestic slave," and deplored housework as "barbarously unproductive, petty, nerve-racking, stultifying, and crushing drudgery." He also derided proletarian husbands who shirked their chores, saying, "The husband must not content himself with 'assisting.' He must rather do his share…" in cleaning and caring for children. This radicalism was carried on into the constitutions of the Eastern Bloc nations after the communist victory in the Second World War, replacing reactionary papal pro-housewife hegemony in places like Lithuania, Hungary, and Poland.

But though these sorts of factors might have informed global psycho-geo-tic perceptions somewhat, affiliating the USSR with "mother" was largely irrational. Psycho-geo-tics is, after all, an unconscious, emotional, and little-understood process which has to do with people's animal or "primal" instincts. These are just largely unused psychic detritus: reflexes and superstitions inherited from genetic survival programming, developed over millions of years of living in swamps, caves, nests, pyramids, alien spacecraft, basement apartments, and piles of dung. The USSR was identified psycho-geo-tically as "mother" because its foreign and domestic behavior resonated with the primitive psyche, which saw it as embodying the "mother" archetype: authoritarian, furtive, implacable, cruel, and irrational. The USSR, despite its moral mission, was prone to girlish spite and paranoia, as witnessed by Stalin's bitchy purging of various party rivals, whom he named "degenerate Bukharinite double-dealers," "Trotskyite Whiteguard gang of assassins," "contemptible lackeys of the fascists," and "Whiteguard pygmies whose strength was no more than that of a gnat."

In religious systems—or "mythology"—from time immemorial, the "mother goddess" is simultaneously life giver and destroyer. For example, Ishtar, Cybele, Freya, and Devi are all mother goddesses of sex and fertility—and of death and destruction—for each of their highly disparate cultures. The Soviet Union, with its lively paradox of radical reform/populist rhetoric combined with deadly "Red terror," crept unconsciously into this dualistic psycho-geo-tic role.

In the murky marshland of the hominid's brain core then, the symbol of the hammer and the sickle represents the earth's primal progeny (in Marxist argot, "the proletariat") whose fertility and virility have been awoken by Mother's magical tools of reaping and forging. These tools are also the sex organs at play with one another. But this hammer and sickle are also recognized as symbols of destruction, used to rend and crush. The flag of the Soviet Union, with its hammer, sickle, and cloth, is like a rock-paper-scissors game in which all destructive options are represented simultaneously: a maelstrom of malevolent energy that menaces its opponent but also threatens to destroy itself. Marx's appropriation of Hegelian "dialectics"—resolution through thesis/antithesis contradiction—also refers to the schizo-sex-death-mother matrix latent in communism.

That the communist system spurs fecundity is witnessed by the remarkable transformation of the Russian and Chinese feudal economies and their rejection of sex-hating Christo-Judaic-Mohammedan dogma (religions remarkable for their absence of a female deity). The USSR, despite its chronic poverty, took pains to provide its children with their basic needs—hence the sneering characterization as "nanny states" or "nurturers" by conservatives when speaking of socialist governments (or, pejoratively, "welfare states").

Such semantics are highly illuminating. The self-righteousness and didacticism of communists, often compared to religious zealotry, is really the entitled intransigence of motherhood. Stalin's terror can be seen as a kind of postpartum depression scenario with the mother, after the shock of birth (revolution), trying to destroy her young (both revolutionaries and counterrevolutionaries).

Because the USSR was psycho-geo-tically connected to a mother archetype or mother-sex-death goddess figure, its official enemy automatically became the inverse of that character in the unconscious imagination, so the

USA became a kind of male champion god in the vein of Hermes or Thoth, phallic deities of commerce and mystery.

IV. FATHER

Despite (or because of) the mother's authoritarian nurturing and condescending concern, the child identifies with this hermetic-USA-father figure. Vainglorious, anti-intellectual, cunning, glamorous—he is a "hero" archetype, the Arcadian psycho-pomp who undertakes daring missions, transgresses boundaries, and guards secret knowledge. Conquest, glory, alchemy, and acquisition are his creed.

Elitism, race theory, and numeric esoterica are the specters behind his proclaimed money ideology. The horror of the so-called third world is the result of his serial philandering: exploitation that he shirks with no recognition of responsibility. He voraciously consumes everything he sees. His concubines, or "client states," dream they can rehabilitate him, or "save his soul." Religion or mysticism is his domain, a tool for social control and perhaps also a form of sublimated guilt: a fascination and attraction to the alien and unthinkable concept of self-sacrifice. Though this character seems distasteful, his audacity and entitled arrogance are considered "sexy."

To the repressed psycho-geo-tic pattern-recognition instincts of the bipedal fleshpot, his flag, the "stars and bars," shows the rungs of a ladder in a prison covered with blood. The night sky can be seen through the window in the upper left-hand corner—a tease of liberty. If one looks very closely, one can see the father's private helicopter flying past "Orion's belt."

Not coincidentally to this latent gender motif, the October Revolution occurred in simultaneity with the global suffragette/feminist movement.

While the plutocracy of the West is often referred to as an "old boys' club," the USSR initiated the aforementioned radical women's rights reforms with the Bolshevik victory, including divorce on demand, abortion rights, and even a sci-fi attempt to abolish housework and the family.

The Soviet Union's rapid industrialization and vigorous response to the West's arms race was a testimonial to the Russians' sense of themselves as the serially abused victim of their historic capitalist-imperialist exploiters. Joseph Stalin, speaking in 1931 to the First Conference of Industrial Managers, explained, "One feature of the history of old Russia was the continual beatings she suffered because of her backwardness. She was beaten by the Mongol khans. She was beaten by the Turkish beys. She was beaten by the Swedish feudal lords. She was beaten by the Polish and Lithuanian gentry. She was beaten by the British and French capitalists. She was beaten by the Japanese barons. All beat her—because of her backwardness...

"But we do not want to be beaten. No, we refuse to be beaten!

"We are fifty or a hundred years behind the advanced countries. We must make good this distance in ten years. Either we do it, or we shall go under . . ."

So, though Russia was Mother, it was no longer the hobbled tsarist consort, entangled with the West as a bullied partner, but the "Soviet" divorcée of considerable willfulness. This woman's liberation was a challenge to male domination and threatened the traditional distribution of power. The tsarist mother had served the father well in her time and bore him fruit, but this new insubordination could not stand.

While rapprochement was always sought by the much weaker Soviet side throughout the Cold War in an attempt at cooperation and reconciliation (such a state of harmony between oppositional male and female forces was called "syzygy" by Jung, and "entente" by the political class), the USA needed a public example to be set.

She would have to be destroyed—though the necromancers in Western intelligence understood the profound effect such an event would have on the world's population. First, a softening-up was needed.

V. PROGRAMMING

Psychologists employed by the Western spy agencies understood the psycho-geo-tics represented by the global ideological schism and attempted to exploit these latent feelings through the arts. Cultural propaganda at the height of the Cold War ritually featured mother-death in television programs aimed at children such as *My Three Sons, Family Affair, The Andy Griffith Show,* and *The Courtship of Eddie's Father,* among others.

There is almost always a manservant (e.g., the femme "Uncle French" or the butch "Uncle Charley") in these televised scenarios who performs the mother's traditional job of mothering, but who noticeably forgoes her overbearing and controlling manner. The implication in the aforementioned scenarios is clear: the murder of the mother is desirable and a necessary step toward the child's liberation.

This subordinate "Uncle" figure presages the eventual collaborative style of the mother's killing. It is never explained who exactly has murdered the missing mother on these programs, and the characters never discuss or question the tragedy. However, it is always explicit that without her, existence is of the magical variety exemplified on television.

The death of the socialistic superpower is this desirable wife-mother murder. It is achieved with the collusion of the Uncle figure—China—who was once Mother Russia's lover (Stalin-Mao pact), but who, feeling jealous and angry about his inability to control her (Khrushchev's denouncement of Stalin, leading to fissure with China at the Cominform), conspires with her archenemy/ex-husband (the USA, in the temporal form of Nixon) in order to kill her (the two-front confrontation which bankrupted the USSR).

Uncle China then mimics Father's worst exploitive and avaricious tendencies while appropriating Mother's authoritarian irrational streak. Though he is now business partners with the blithe and hedonistic husband/father, he also dreams of destroying him eventually and it seems certain that he will.

VI. POOR WINNER

Of course, there is also an element of matricide in all of this. Just as each election witnesses the USA as death-cult, casting its ballots for self-immolation, apocalypse, and the decline of the dollar, Eastern Europe's children, tired of their mother's moodiness, purposefully left the door ajar in a considered criminal accessorization.

As Mother lay dying, the father's first act was to molest them, just as Mother had warned that he would. She never told them, though, that he would film the act for money. To assuage the guilt they feel for collaborating with their mother's killer, they allow themselves a disingenuous gullibility, believing the father's coital promise to phone and send chocolates. They call him pet names and brag about their relationship with him.

The rest of the world, having already been deflowered by him ages ago, is not impressed but understands. They are, however, deeply

disturbed by the father's fondling of his es-
tranged wife's children. His vengeful pleasure
in exploiting them is evident. In victory he
has proved to be a "poor winner." Meanwhile,
with a newfound zest for masochism, Russia
and the former socialist republics pledge alle-
giance to the father's heroic hypermacho mythology, replacing their communal ideology
with his mystic blend of reaction, elitism, racism, and nationalism. Right-wing "skinheads"
abound, religion is back, and feminism has
been abandoned. This cloying copy ideologiz-
ing is typical of nations in defeat (i.e., postwar
Japan's rehabilitation as a US-style capitalist
economy), but pathetic in this case since the
father's *weltanschauung* is secretly based on a
race system whereby the Slavs are subhumans,
targeted for extermination.

While the Russians mimic the worst
traits of their usurper, the USA does a crude
burlesque of its victim in a perverse identity
switch, a ritual akin to a soldier trying on the
hat of an enemy "kill." Hence the recent appropriation in the US of a Soviet-style kitsch

adoration of public servants, like firemen, paramedics, and the military.

Though officially murdered and buried in the yard, the Soviet still lives in the collective psyche, a repressed memory of the mother which haunts both her killers and the world's now-defenseless tots. Her death leaves a yawning void, a missing champion to invoke or petition against Father's serial abuse. This is what has caused cosmic depression (PSD syndrome) and the fantastic popularity of newfangled antidepressant pills. Meanwhile, without a foil, Father has "gone to seed," abandoning former pretenses of idealism and lashing out in delusional fits.

The discovery of psycho-geo-tics by the US government and the manipulation of its latent force were instrumental in engineering the destruction of the USSR and the enslavement of the globe. The utilization of psycho-geo-tic power wasn't confined to that global conflagration, though, but is conjured still through so-called culture. The Cold War was, in a sense, an illuminating macrocosm of the conflict we all fight every day.

Dracula: The Fallen Race

VAMPIRISM &
VAMPIROLOGY

Besides serving as the foil for *fin de siècle*–era costume drama soft-core pornography (à la *Vampyros Lesbos*), the vampire figure is typically utilized in legend and literature as sexual metaphor.

He or she, an undead cipher, is invoked to symbolize foreign philanderer (Hammer horror), pubescent possession (*The Lost Boys*), erotic deviant (Lestat), or whatever the strategic or psychological demands of the author or culture.

He seems damned for eternity to be an all-purpose metaphorical sex device, the hapless agent of identity politicians everywhere.

But the vampire's modern literary origin, with Bram Stoker's gothic classic *Dracula*, published in 1897, tells a different tale.

The book's appearance coincided with the Victorian age's obsession with genealogy, Social Darwinism, Nietzsche, and eugenics, and was in fact meant to summarize and organize these concerns into a coherent ideology. An examination of Dracula therefore illuminates much regarding the outlook and intentions of the Western moneyed class over the last century.

Stoker's vampire was actually based on the historical figure Vlad Tepes of the Knightly "Order of the Dragon" (*Draco* meaning "dragon," hence "Dracula").

In the fifteenth century, Vlad was the "Voivode" or Count of Wallachia and Transylvania in what is now Romania, a state originally founded by Frankish crusaders in 1204 after their sack of Constantinople. Named for Rome and intended as a Vatican usurper of Orthodox Byzantine power, Romania was nestled against that Eastern Christian empire, an entity hated and envied by the crusaders for its wealth, learning, and perceived decadent sophistication.

This original Romania was short-lived, destroyed by its Byzantine nemesis within the century and then overrun by various Eastern invaders. It subsequently served as the gateway to Europe from the eastern Steppes, homeland of the Huns, Magyars, Mongols, and other warrior horse tribes.

Despite the resulting turmoil, Romania retained the Catholic character of its crusaders' political delineation, an island of Vatican influence in a sea of Orthodox, Islamic, and elsewise exotic tribes.

By the 1400s, the region's various feudal states were Christianity's front line against Ottoman expansion after the Turkic sultan crushed Byzantium and his armies crashed furiously northward. Count Vlad Dracula gained historic notoriety warring against these Muslim Turks, the archfoe of Christian Europe, as they answered the European Crusades with a bigger and badder jihad of their own.

In Bram Stoker's story, Dracula is still in Transylvania after five hundred years, residing in his castle as an aristocratic undead. He must suck the blood from his victims to maintain eternal "life" as a spectral demon. His targets are typically beautiful, upper-class young women.

Although the vampire is nominally held in ill regard, the book's popularity and the volumes it has inspired reveal that his character—the immortal, insatiable lothario with a blood obsession—is actually a secret protagonist whom the reader is intended to empathize with.

And such was the author's design. Because *Dracula* is not a simple Gothic fairy tale, but an allegorical manifesto. And while Dracula is a dissembler, he is not the horny teen or the gay blade of modern pulp, but the Race in crisis, the now-sullied Caucasoid superpeople on a constant search for "untainted blood," a.k.a. pure genetic stock, to maintain immortality. The blood of Dracula's obsession is his bloodline: the genealogy of his brides and tribe. He sucks the "clean" DNA from the virginal or nubile girl, who represents unspoiled lineage, and then begets them as vampire children, the Dracula offspring.

Dracula, the Romanian defender of the faith, was chosen as subject because of his ancient role in protecting Mother Europe from Turkic insemination; the author is warning of what can befall even the most warlike and ethnophobic tribe.

In Stoker's time, Transylvania, once part of Roman Dacia and then Romania, was a province of the ethnically diverse Austro-Hungarian Empire, ill-esteemed by nationalist ideologues and particularly despised by racialists. German-speaking Austrians such as Guido Von List (and later Adolf Hitler) were among the most vociferous German nationalists and propounded the most acute racial philosophies. They longed for unification with their fatherland and despised the random polyglot of the dual monarchy.

Protagonist Jonathan Harker's travel diary, which serves as the narrative for much of *Dracula*, is full of imperialist ethnic observations about the mongrelized masses who inhabit the hinterlands surrounding Castle Dracula. As an Englishman, Harker is fascinated by the various Servians, Székelys, Cszeks, and other exotic beasts he sees. "The strangest figures we saw were the Slovaks, who were more barbarian than the rest . . . they are however, I am told, very harmless and rather wanting in natural self-assertion," he says, with the colonial condescension that has endeared masochists everywhere to all things British. He goes on: "The women looked pretty, except when you got near them . . ."

Dracula has hired the archbourgeois Harker as broker to assist his impending move to London. Through indoctrination by various civil tomes and travel books, Dracula has become an Anglophile; "through [these books] I have come to know your great England; and to know her is to love her," he tells Harker.

He must move to London from his ancient home in the East because it has been dirtied by miscegenation and interbreeding with Slavs, Magyars, Wallachs, and other *untermensch*.

In Transylvania he is forced to feast on (inter-breed with) common Slavic peasantry.

Meanwhile, he professes his "love" for England, imbuing the country with the characteristics of a person, in a way typical of that era's nationalists.

He "loves" the blood of England, the achievements of its pure and vigorous children, and desires them sexually for his own genetic ends.

Like Harker, he is obsessed with racial origins: "We Székelys have a right to be proud, for in our veins flows the blood of many brave races who fought as the lion fights, for lordship. Here, in the whirlpool of European races, the Ugric tribe bore down from Iceland the fighting spirit which Thor and Wodin gave them, which their Berserkers displayed to such fell intent on the seaboards of Europe, aye, and of Asia and Africa too, till the peoples thought that the werewolves themselves had come."

Dracula, though Eastern European, claims descent from Viking tribes and invokes the Norse gods, racialist symbols of Nordic-Aryan purity. This was a common conceit of turn-of-the-century white supremacist mythology, that the great peoples of history were all of Aryan-Nordic ancestries, ultimately spawned from the land of Hyperborea, near the Arctic. Interbreeding with ethnic flotsam over the ages had unfortunately caused them to lose their various superpowers, which had once included telepathy.

Dracula goes on: "Here, too, when they [his Viking ancestors] came, they found the Huns, whose warlike fury had swept the earth like a living flame, till the dying peoples held that in their veins ran the blood of those old witches, who, expelled from Scythia, had mated with the devils in the desert. Fools, fools! What devil or what witch was ever so great as Attila, whose blood is in these veins?" He holds up his arms. "Is it a wonder that we were a conquering race; that we were proud; that when the Magyar, the Lombard, the Avar, the Bulgar, or the Turk poured his thousands on our frontiers, we drove them back?"

Thus the pure Viking blood has been made

merciless and cannibalistic through its blending with the savage, Oriental Hun: a most fearsome racial brew!

The Voivode has grand plans for London. As a member of a fallen race, dirtied by mongrelization and therefore "undead," he is just a ghostly specter of former glory. Using Britain's premium Anglo-Saxon genetic stock, he will produce exemplary white progeny, infuse himself with purity, and live forever. He will take a young English thing back to his Eastern kingdom where they will resuscitate and then strengthen the lapsed bloodline. He will attempt purification through backward eugenics breeding farms in an "Aryan transfusion," the same tactic the Nazis would attempt in Scandinavia forty years later in their desire to recreate the mythological superrace of their fantasies.

Dracula resides on earth transported from his home in Transylvania because, in racialist thought, a people or race are not just *from* their homeland, they are *of* their homeland, as much as the trees, rocks, and streams. (Israelis and

Palestinians are some of the modern devotees of this arcane racial conceit.)

The cross that repels him is a symbol of the Semitic religion that he despises, a close relative to the Islamicism he once saved the white race from. As the symbol of Christ's martyrdom and of Christ's pan-tribal invitation to goyim for initiation into the religion of the Jews, the cross also represents the death of the genetic ideal expounded by Judaism, in favor of equalizing Christian evangelism.

Christianity is therefore horrific to Dracula as it was to the elite SS troops who were initiated into the pagan esoterica of Third Reich ideology forty years later.

Hitler's collusion with the Vatican and the papal sponsorship of the "ratline," which ferried SS Nazis to safety in South America, reveals the Vatican's own bizarre pagan and supremacist leanings.

The sunlight that can destroy Dracula represents the attention which liberal enlightenment philosophy and modernist pluralism will wreak on the eugenic program. Therefore this mission must be undertaken in subterfuge, at night and with much dissembling. Garlic, representing ethnic food from the Mediterranean region, frightens him especially as it symbolizes the seductive power of pan-nationalism embodied at the time by the Ottoman and Russian empires.

Note that the British model of imperialism was not the expansive Ottoman or Russian model whereby the mother culture absorbs the conquered peoples, unified under a common paradigm (such as a particular language or religion), but a "divide-and-conquer" strategy in which various subjects' ethnicities were actually amplified, exacerbated, ranked, and set against one another even as they were corralled together within new contrived nation states.

Though Stoker supports poor Dracula's racialist quest, he has him destroyed in the end by the Dutch vampire killer Van Helsing, with the help of Harker, the bourgeois Englishman; Quincy Morris, the Texan; and Seward, a modernized English nobleman.

Van Helsing declares, "The Draculas were a

great and noble *race*," yet the Dutch, English, and American vampire killers represent the new Masonic bourgeois powers which will guarantee whiteness in the future.

Dracula's aristocratic fogeyism has proven insufficient in defending Nordic-Aryan supremacy from its foreign threats, as evidenced by the myriad tribes which pollute the lands around Castle Dracula.

The hammer and stake which are ceremoniously used to destroy him represent the industrial prowess of the New West against the lascivious degeneracy of Dracula's orientalized royalism. Stoker, though a racialist imperial apologist, echoes Marx in this dialectical displacement of feudalism by the industrial-imperialist middle class.

Of course, as vampire killer Seward hammers his vampire wife Lucy through the heart, he is compared favorably by the author with Thor, insinuating that the industrial might of the West has its root in Aryan-Nordic magic and ingenuity.

In fact, Seward's presence as token nobleman is intended to alleviate aristocratic fears that this allegorical manifesto seeks to displace them.

Stoker reassures them that this is not so, while he simultaneously cautions them to move with the times and embrace the vitality of their mercantile bourgeois counterparts.

The vampire's finicky palate, usually interpreted as a gourmet sexual appetite, honed over many centuries, is a more complex thing than mere libidinality. It is the late-nineteenth-century occult revival fused with that era's social Darwinist rationalization of racial superiority: a cunning hybrid of the dominant European upper-class fascinations of the time. To resuscitate his own bloodline, Dracula must draw on British blood (the empire was at its height then) because the British are the dominant strain of the Caucasian superrace.

The ideology represented in *Dracula* found its acme of overground expression in Germany with the Nazi Party, but it was not new then nor has it disappeared. Racial supremacy is, in subterfuge, at the heart of each decision made by the satanic functionaries of the "Western" powers. Though the principle victims are Africans, Asians, and Semites, the Slavic people are also special objects of contempt and targeted as *untermensch*. The Nazis and their allies killed tens of millions of Soviet civilians in their colonial war of racial extermination (1941–45).

The US-NATO subsidy of the Catholic Croats against the Orthodox Serbs is just one example that the Vatican and the West are still waging the crusade against these despised Easterners. In WWII, of course, the Nazis sponsored the Croatians as an Aryan people while the Serbs, as Slavs, were condemned to death. Himmler also declared the Serbian province Kosovo as an Albanian state and managed the Serb slaughter there with special Albanian SS troops. Hitler's Balkan dream was never realized, though, until the Clinton era when Madison Avenue marketed race war as "humanitarian."

While Stoker's *Dracula* story specifically

addresses the genetic concerns of the European upper classes, vampirism—an ancient legend shared by many different cultures—is also a mass movement, enjoyed by every conquering race.

Coke Adds Life

THE BLOODY LATTE

Vampirism As a Mass Movement

The penchant for a culture to imbibe drinks and drugs en masse, in a collective ritual-orgy, is a phenomenon which transcends mere fashion.

This, in itself, is unworthy of remark; the quest for transcendence through intoxication is as old as history itself. The cultural particularity of the proclivity is what is striking: the strange uniformity of every epoch's beverage cult.

Personal taste amounts to little; instead, for each era, there's a distinctive mass hysteria for the imbibing of a particular beverage or substance.

The drinks at this juncture in American history are indisputably coffee from Starbucks and the vodka of Absolut. The popularity of these drinks stems from their value as symbolic war booty from recent conquests. A culture's adopted beverage represents the blood of its vanquished foe.

Drink is transubstantiation à la the Catholic cannibalism of Christ's blood and body. The smell of coffee is the odor of the Sandinista hospital, bodies maimed by Contra bombs. Ice-cold vodka is the blood of the Russians, raped and murdered by capitalism.

And so it has been through history. Each imperial culture imports a liquid memento from their vanquished foe to serve as a totem of their power and glory. Tea, the Englishman's beverage, is falling out of favor as their neocolonial hold on the subcontinent wavers. For two centuries the English supped on their well-steeped leaves and tasted the sweat of the slaves in the empire. Now, tea is for old mums, while beer-swilling "lads" form the visible majority. The British love their beer; a cold pint brings fond memories of dead Germans, falling out of the sky in the Battle of Britain.

Beer first attained great popularity in America immediately after the First World War, when the US had tipped the scale against the Kaiser in the last days of the conflict. That war had been highly unpopular to a then-isolationist nation, with American involvement cynically contrived by Anglophiles in government. The war transformed the country profoundly, much to the consternation of its activists.

The women who had raged for abolition and suffrage now turned their eyes to alcohol, successfully banishing it in 1920. Prohibition, then, was unconsciously a moral crusade against imperialism and the blood sucking and chest beating that followed the Treaty of Versailles. Of course, beer made a comeback, especially after the Depression hit and veterans needed to boost self-esteem by slurping the entrails of the wretched Kraut. A cold beer in a bar with one's buddies brought one's thoughts to the bread lines in Berlin, with all its one-legged soldiers.

Beer was big in Germany a thousand years

earlier, when King Otto had pushed back the Slavic Wend and Magyar interlopers from the East. For the German, it is essentially the blood of the Slav. Its popularity was reinforced when Frederick the Great struck into the bread basket of Poland, expanding Prussia, a conquest that led to German domination of the continent under Bismarck.

Years later, to invoke the German's blood-lust, an Austrian man named Hitler held meetings in Munich beer halls, and cited the loss of those wheat fields, now occupied by Slavs.

When Hitler rose to power, after the "Beer Hall Putsch," he allied himself with the Italian dictator Mussolini, who dreamed of imperial glory in Africa. The Italian conquest of Ethiopia, the birthplace of coffee, resulted in the espresso craze in Italy. During the Second World War, each Italian soldier carried an espresso maker in his mess kit. The Starbucks aesthetic—garish, fascistic murals combined with futurist mechanization of the workforce and absurdist shouting—can be traced to Mussolini.

America's love of coffee has always been tied to the affection for conquest. Coffee fueled the "winning of the West" and the usurpation of the former colonies of Spain at the turn of the century. Guatemala, El Salvador, Nicaragua, Colombia, etc., have all been virtual colonies since then, with frequent US-armed interventions to ensure servitude.

These nations constitute the mainstay of our coffee supply, and much blood has been spilled to maintain it. Coffee was the blood of the Indian, and gave one the adrenal rush needed to achieve "manifest destiny." Coffee was "Joe," as in Joe Nobody or John Doe, as the racist dehumanization of the native peoples refuted any necessity for their identification.

This name was changed to "Java" in the 1960s, when the US helped install the dictator Suharto in Indonesia; he murdered so many of his subjects at the behest of insecure multinationals. Although this was a proxy war, not directly fought by the US, coffee's taste still reflects the power imparted by the struggle. Its flavor was enriched and it grew in popularity.

Whether Indian or Indonesian, coffee was the blood of the vanquished and it tasted good.

Now, in the global economy, coffee is grown across the entire subjugated third world. When Starbucks sells a bag of beans, it's always marked with the region from whence it sprang, making the consumer an imperial cannibal connoisseur.

Coca-Cola is another toast of imperial conquest; it initially drew its flavor from the coca plant from Central America, but switched to another regional flavor (tamarind root) when this was outlawed. Coca-Cola's ascendancy coincided with the Spanish-American War and the annexation of Puerto Rico, Cuba, etc. It was often mixed with rum, the sugar-based flavor of those very islands.

Coke was provided to all American soldiers during the Second World War as a way to "blood" the army. Coke plants in Germany changed their trade-name to Fanta, so as to deflect charges of corporate two-timing in the war effort. Fanta was orange, a flavor homage to the smashed Republican army in Spain, where the German army had first honed their killing skills. When a German drank an orange pop, he was gnawing the jugular of an anarcho-syndicalist in Valencia.

Vodka is the refined fruit of the peasant's potato. Under the tsars, Russia's border relentlessly expanded, from the Baltic to the Black Sea, and then on to the Pacific. Conquered people, impressed into serfdom, were manifest in the vodka drink favored by the Russian ruling class, both before the execution of the tsar and then later with Stalin.

Vodka can actually be made from a variety of grains and fruits, appropriate to the vast and varied lands of Muscovite conquest. For the Russians, this drink, the blood of Swedes, Finns, Lithuanians, Ukrainians, Uzbeks, and Khazars, became suddenly, under the creed of communist internationalism, the celebration of fratricide. This accounts for the existential mania and depression that famously accompanies modern Russian drunkenness.

With the conclusion of the Cold War, and Russia under the yoke of exploitive capitalism, vodka is more and more beloved by Americans, who gulp it smugly as proof positive of their power to sculpt the earth. Sweden, the traditional nemesis of tsarist Russia, is the producer par excellence of the trophy drink.

As we can see, the cultural specificity of the blood represented by a drink is contingent on the race or nationality of the person drinking. So, while a German drinking a beer would be enjoying the life force of the Slav, an American popping a "Bud" would be eating the guts of that same German man. Similarly, a toast of expatriate brand "Bacardi" rum is a celebration of the assassination of Che in Bolivia, while a splash of "Habana Club," the Cuban national brand, is the bloody froth from the surf at the Bay of Pigs.

And so it goes: tequila's worm is the dead Yankee at the Alamo, as *gusano* or "worm" is the Latin revolutionaries' name for the *Yanqui* imperialist. Even the introduction of Perrier to America coincided with the death of the nationalist de Gaulle and the subsequent compliance of France with NATO. (The boycott of an intransigent and undefeated foe's imported foodstuffs follows a similar repressed logic, as with Cuban rum or French wine during the Iraq War.) Wine was championed by the Gauls upon the disintegration of its drinkers, the imperial Roman occupiers. The Romans had snatched it from their Greek competitor, whose empire they had eclipsed, while the Greek slave states begat their wine from the stamping feet of their war captives, and so on, ad infinitum, to the prehistoric dawn of life on the planet.

Food rituals have always been centered on hierarchy and power. The cow is ingested because it is essentially defenseless against us. We assert our primacy over nature by ingesting it in a gory ceremony of flesh chewing. The animals we admire are felines and canines, bears and eagles: predators like us. This is an ancient warrior's ethic, echoed in the American craze for Nazi memorabilia. The milk of the breast is the first liquid imbibed by the newborn child. The baby learns that his mewing automatically summons the mother, whereupon she administers the juice of subjugation from her teat. Therefore the taste of liquid is psychically paralleled with subjugation and enslavement even in the semiconscious baby state.

Once again, while Stoker's *Dracula* story per se addresses the genetic concerns of the European upper classes, vampirism—an ancient legend shared by many different cultures—is also a mass movement, enjoyed by every conquering race.

The Tongue and the Fruit

BEATLES VS. STONES

An Examination of the Schism

I. SYMPATHY FOR THE DEVIL

Everyone knows the 1968 Rolling Stones goof-ball epic "Sympathy for the Devil." Composed in front of Jean-Luc Godard's cameras for the film *One Plus One*, the song betrays the voodoo inculcation of their friend Dr. John, whose *Gris-Gris* album had become an underground hit that year. The Stones had liberally cribbed from the swampy black-magick sound of that record, particularly on their song "Gimme Shelter." Indeed, it seems that only by borrowing Dr. John's identity could the Stones break from slavishly aping the Beatles' innovations.

Initially, the song seems an unlikely choice for Godard, with its theme of Satan through history wreaking havoc on the status quo. The lyrics actually seem to propose that the person responsible for murdering the Kennedys, Jesus Christ, and Tsar Nicholas were, in fact, one and the same: the song's singer, who is apparently the Devil.

Godard had already engaged in an impressive flurry of filmmaking that year, having just made *La Chinoise, Le Gai Savoir,* and *Weekend.*

His films had become more polemic, more didactic, and less beholden to narrative. He had cast his lot in unequivocally with the revolutionary movements happening across the globe, in Vietnam, Cuba, and Paris.

La Chinoise sympathetically follows a Maoist cell of Parisian youths as they commit murder in the name of class war. *Weekend* has a bourgeois woman joining a band of hippie-cannibal guerrillas in the forest to eat her husband. *Le Gai Savoir* posits a boy and girl making film from a new paradigm. The film *One Plus One* has three distinct episodes, the centerpiece being a cinema verité exposition of the Rolling Stones in the studio, trying out endless musical approaches for their new song, "Sympathy for the Devil."

As all manner of instruments are auditioned; the one constant is Mick Jagger's vocal, which never mutates at all.

What would Godard's intent be, to painstakingly document this bit of rock 'n' roll fluff? The lyrics actually equate the killing of the tsar and the Nazi conquest of Europe as the same man's handiwork, meaning in short that Bolshevism = Nazism. The song also seems to suggest that JFK, the man responsible for the American invasions of Vietnam and Cuba, is akin to Christ, the song's narrator's other victim.

As this seems profoundly inconsistent with Godard's Maoist viewpoint, a reexamination of the song's content is in order.

While Godard worked in the mostly academic world of film theory and art concerns, the Stones were employed by American pop radio. Though English by birth, the rock 'n' roll band lived and died at the whim of the American market, which was influenced enormously by disc jocks and commercial television. As in any hegemony, the artist who chooses to say something that is unpopular or verboten risks dismissal. Under Stalin, it was the archipelago; under capitalism, neglect and thus artistic death.

In a pop art form, insignificance surpasses death in horror, as the neglected worker actually labors for his competitors, producing ideas and songs to be resold by those who have access to radio and promotion. "Sympathy for the Devil"'s chorus and theme, for example, had been lifted directly from The Satans' song "Makin' Deals," an obscure LA garage tune no one ever heard.

Because of the nature of this highly ideological and money-driven medium through which the Rolling Stones lived and expressed themselves, ideas (and ideals) had to be shrouded and concealed, as has so often been the case throughout art's history.

"Sympathy for the Devil" never actually announces that it is sung by the Devil. It merely asks the listener, *"Can you guess my name?"*

after the singer regales us with stories of his various exploits. The title of the song could be interpreted quite literally, that the song's singer is sympathetic to the archetype "Devil" or "Lucifer" (the perennial outsider), who's cast from heaven (society) by God (the power structure) for outside views. Read this way, the acts of the song's protagonist are, though widely considered antisocial, actually positive.

> *I was round when Jesus Christ had his moment of doubt and pain.*

This alludes to Christ's momentary reflection on his earthly insignificance, a brief return to the sanity which preceded his "son of God" megalomania.

> *Made damn sure that Pilate washed his hands and sealed his fate.*

Without Christ's supposed crucifixion, there would have been no martyrdom, and no burgeoning Christian movement to eventually unify Europe after spurring the disintegration of the Roman Empire. The Jews couldn't do it as they weren't an evangelical sect, and Zoroastrianism was too hard to pronounce.

> *stuck around St. Petersburg, when I saw it*
> *was time for a change / Killed the tsar and*
> *his ministers, Anastasia screamed in vain.*

This lyric discusses the Bolshevik termination of the Romanov bloodline, and their subsequent changing of that city's name. These were positive developments for Russia, despite Disney's revisionist claims otherwise.

> *I rode a tank, held a general's rank, when*
> *the blitzkrieg raged and the bodies stank.*

This never says what side the general in question fought for, merely that he rode in a tank while the Nazis conducted genocide. The *bodies stank* reference leads us to Russia, where Nazi cruelty was at its worst, so the general is probably Russian tank commander Zhukov, who defeated the Germans at Stalingrad and Kursk, turning the tide of the Second World War.

> *I shouted out, "Who killed the Kennedys?"*
> *when after all it was you and me.*

During VH1's roundup of the one hundred greatest pop songs, Charlie Watts comments on this song, saying simply, "controversial lyrics": this is what he was referring to. The Rolling Stones are supporting the unpopular lone-gunman theory here, saying that Oswald was not a stooge, but an actual socialist with a rifle, who killed the president as an act of conscience. JFK was, after all, a dangerous idiot who nearly blew up the world. The *you and me* lyric is Mick as Oswald singing directly to poor CIA mind-control victim Sirhan Sirhan and all the various federal agencies who helped murder RFK.

As the song progresses, we see now that its protagonist is not the "Devil," but the Marxist idea of dialecticism through history, the inevitable changes which lead us from exploitation—first by kings under feudalism, and then by the bourgeoisie under capitalism—to a socialist government and communist society: a process called "historical materialism." We see why Jean-Luc Godard employed the Stones, despite their seeming incongruence with his trajectory at the time. This is the reason for this particular song being played over and over in the film, with the lyric as the only constant.

"Sympathy for the Devil" was released on the LP *Beggars Banquet*. The record cover featured a filthy toilet bedecked with graffiti. Released in the wake of *Sgt. Pepper's, Piper at the Gates of Dawn, S.F. Sorrow,* and in the same year as *Tommy*, the album was expected to have a cohesive presentation, and not just be a collection of songs. The Rolling Stones were nothing if not conscious of fashion and the market. The theme or concept they chose for *Banquet* is unmistakably Marxist, from the LP title to the songs "Salt of the Earth," "Factory Girl," and "Street Fighting Man."

In the graffiti on the cover are written the

words *Bob Dylan's Dream,* with an arrow going to the flusher. This is a pointed dismissal of Dylan's then-recent "politics are a drag" stance. If Dylan's dream was mere hedonist escapism, the Stones considered it sewage. As the song closes, Mick cries out, again and again, *"Can you guess my name?"* He seems to beg us, stridently at first, then desperately, finally incoherently. And no wonder—no one ever guessed his name. It was "Historical Materialism."

II. BACK IN THE USSR

The Beatles' *White Album* (1968) has caused much speculation on the part of hippie-Nazis like Manson, who felt that "Helter Skelter" was code for an oncoming race war, and "Piggies" an indictment of the bourgeoisie. Inspecting the lyrics, we see little evidence to support these fantasies, which leads us to suspect the whole "Family" phenomenon as an FBI/Agency ruse: gory sensationalism intended to discredit the burgeoning peace movement.

The idea that The Beatles may have wanted to convey serious, even subversive messages through a pop medium is quite possible, though. In the wake of Leonard Bernstein and the critical elite trumpeting their *Sgt. Pepper's* album, The Beatles were certainly aware of their influence on culture. Like no one before or since, they simultaneously bewitched the intelligentsia and the teenybops. Paul McCartney spoke candidly of their cultural position, likening his group to revolutionary composers such as Igor Stravinsky. They made daring announcements about their use of illegal psychedelics and aversion to the Vietnam War.

The Beatles had come up fast in this period, initially indulging in the carnality of success, then, disillusioned, going on a spiritual retreat to India.

Returning from India, the group started their work on what would be called *The White Album*.

The song "Back in the USSR" seems to address this disenchantment with their perceived hollowness of materialist society.

Outwardly, the tune is clever, a spoof on The Beach Boys' trademarked postwop vocals and patriotic lyrics. The song may qualify, along with "Happiness Is a Warm Gun," as one of the first postmodern rock 'n' roll songs, with its self-conscious deconstruction of the surf genre using seemingly ironic lyrics. Paul McCartney was actually buddies with Beach Boys maestro Brian Wilson (both men were left-handed, bass-playing Geminis), so the spoof could be a tribute, or perhaps something entirely different. Perhaps politics, maybe even prophecy.

The lyrics seem especially poignant now, with the wretched dissolution of Russia after the fall of communism, and the wholesale surrender of that country to exploitation by foreign "investors." *"Back in the USSR. . ."* the song says, *"you don't know how lucky you are."* The chorus seems prophetic, but maybe Paul was merely canny, having spent time in the occupied zone (American/British West Germany) and knowing the allure that Western goods had to the poorer Easterners.

The song begins, strangely enough, in Cuban right-wing expatriate stronghold Miami Beach.

> *Flew in from Miami Beach, B.O.A.C., didn't get to bed last night / On the way the paper bag was on my knee . . . man, I had a dreadful flight.*

The reactionary counterrevolutionaries have so sickened the song's protagonist, he's actually been vomiting. *"I'm back in the USSR!"* he exclaims, overjoyed that he's been delivered from the vulgarian citadel to his beloved Soviet Socialist Republic.

> *Leave it to tomorrow to unpack my case.*

The baubles he's collected at the American mall to impress his proletarian mate have lost their charm, as they're overwhelmed by the beauty of the motherland and the socialist system.

> *Honey, disconnect the phone.*

His attitude betrays an isolationism which goes against Lenin's internationalist doctrine, but here is merely intended to belie any need to communicate with the West.

> Ukraine girls really knock me out...
> Moscow girls make me sing and shout /
> Georgia's always on my mind.

This lyric belies Wilson's declaration about the supremacy of "California girls," which he had carefully outlined in an eponymously titled Beach Boys song. Although the USSR was an ethnically diverse country, the protagonist sees beauty in all its inhabitants.

> Let me hear your balalaikas ringing out,
> Come and keep your comrade warm.

This is a nationalist sentiment, which refutes the rock/guitar craze and Western instrumentation that were sweeping away all cultural nuances in the rest of Europe. After his international touring, McCartney would have well understood rock 'n' roll's cultural impact in spreading capitalist ideology.

Here we see the Stones and The Beatles once again treading the same territory, but in markedly different ways. While "Sympathy" searches through history for examples of dialectic upheaval, The Beatles are actually looking backward from the future onto their own time, warning the Soviets of the folly that will befall them if they are seduced by capitalism. *"You don't know how lucky you are, boy,"* they insist, as they survey the wreckage of modern Russia.

Such an appraisal of this song leads one to examine the other tunes comprising *The White Album*, most notably Lennon's "Revolution," which decries the extremism of particular incendiary groups. One line declares, *"If you go carrying pictures of Chairman Mao / You ain't gonna make it with anyone anyhow."* In lieu of their pro-Soviet posturing earlier on the record, we recognize that this reflects the Sino-Soviet split, which occurred around this time, when Mao was incensed by Khrushchev's denunciation of Stalin. This fissure prompted Nixon's cynical collusion with the Chinese, and the resulting isolation, and eventual defeat, of Russia. Nineteen sixty-eight was also a landmark year of the "Cultural Revolution" in China, which precipitated horrible barbarity against "intellectuals" in the name of agrarianism. The Cultural Revolution of course was Mao's war against a rebellious Communist Party which he replaced with a personality cult based around himself. The "intellectuals" he vilified and destroyed were Soviet-style party apparatchiks.

In Western pop, '68 was similarly the year that "cerebral" psychedelic music was refuted in the name of a "roots" country/blues revival, typified by Creedence, Grateful Dead, Burrito Brothers, etc. This would spell the end of The Beatles, who had essentially invented "intellectual" psychedelia, while it furthered the career of the Stones, who represented the mass proliferation of a rural aesthetic.

The BEATLES VS. STONES dialectic, then,

was actually Lennon/McCartney's industrial Sovietology vs. Mick and Keith's agrarian Maoism, a direct reflection of the intra-Commie ideological conflict of the time. The inability of the revolutionary superpowers to find common ground spelled communism's inevitable dissolution in the face of imperialism, with the absorption of Russia as a new third world, and China's embrace of exploitive capitalist/imperialist tactics.

Their respective ideological surrenders meant the abandonment of smaller nations who relied on their help against neocolonial ingestion by the capitalist "investors." If you think of underground music as occupying the space of a Cuba or Venezuela, and Sony/WEA/et al. representing the USA, the situation seems to still echo the larger conflict.

If only "The Fabs" and "The World's Greatest Rock 'n' Roll Band" could have listened to their own advice, and "Come Together," perhaps it would really have been "alright."

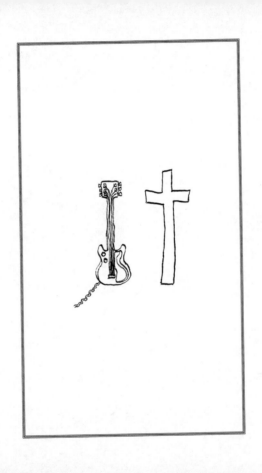

ROCK 'N' ROLLIGION

Christianity will go. It will vanish and shrink. I needn't argue about that; I'm right and I will be proved right. We're more popular than Jesus now.

JOHN LENNON, 1966

Rock 'n' roll has often been compared to a secular religion. The case has also been made again and again, most famously by The Beatles' John Lennon, that this cult of electric guitars and ass shaking has actually replaced Christianity as the so-called West's most dominant and fervent faith.

The charge seemed poignant in the days of "Beatlemania" especially, as the disparate pastimes competed for the population's attention. Now the point is moot, with Christianity assuming the place of an old-timey nostalgia fad, like ham radio or Pez dispensers, its members squawking against impending, self-evident extinction.

Of course, God does enjoy an occasional popularity surge—when the economy tanks or in the event of a worrisome news development—and the populace does genuflect dutifully at His invocation, but most of the time the churches are barren and sad.

Christ has lost, the tired leader of a quaint and cranky cult, whose only role is to reassure the aged or placate the perverse. The rock 'n' roll star has displaced him, a boogie-woogie Antichrist assuming his role as the culture's spiritual leader. The group players are his priests, serving their born-again community from an electric pulpit.

Music's intrinsic spiritual component stands in for the "rapture" associated with religious revival, a component long absent from staid church gatherings, preoccupied now with social decorum. In contrast, the rock congregation can seem gripped by a holy ghost; teenyboppers shriek and faint as "groupies" lend their bodies in flesh sacrifice to the holy man of the hour.

This shift, from Christianity to rock music, is as radical a transformation as was ever initiated by any of the revolutions throughout history. It is an ideological putsch of absolute proportion, occurring without announcement, under the guise of "lifestyle choices" and trends in music.

While Christianity was primarily a tool for the ruling class to convince their impoverished servants to defer pleasure and human rights until a miraculous "afterlife," rock 'n' roll is a capitalist cult, expressing a pleasure principle with an eye to earthly gain and self-obsession. As such, it worships the tenets of the market economy: consumerism, newness, and planned obsolescence.

Therefore, the two movements or religions are diametrically opposed, with one reflecting the repression of the intellectually, economically, and sensually famished, and the other an ideal of absolute excess. In other ways they resemble each other uncannily, possibly because the newer form cannot resist the template of the ancient one.

The startling American metamorphosis from a mostly agrarian, pious, and proudly autonomous population "under God," to a nation of sucker marks mesmerized by their next purchase, was achieved during the great social upheaval which followed the Second World War.

Rock 'n' roll was conceived and constructed in the USA during the postwar period. This is when the old scarcity economy ("laissez-faire" plutocracy), based on a ruling class that starved its subjects, gave way to a new state-guided economy based on consumerism (Keynesianism). American corporations, having worked both sides of the aisle (in a fit of commercial egalitarianism), had made out splendidly. US war bonds and tax dollars had subsidized enormous growth. Gorged on a carte-blanche military budget, industrialists were like pigs in slop, making money hand over fist. And they were intent on perpetuating the fruitful economic model Roosevelt's policies had introduced.

FDR's signature reordering of the economy, called the "New Deal," was modeled on Hitler and Mussolini's "fascist" programs, and was a response to the threat of Marxism. It had succeeded in streamlining industrial America. Mussolini, the inventor of fascism, said: "Fascism should more properly be called corporatism, because it is the merger of state and corporate power," and this description is apt to the USA. The war saw the birth of the so-called military-industrial complex, a model whereby corporations are tax-subsidized to develop products for war but can then keep patents thus developed and sell said product to the "public"—despite that same public's taxes having subsidized the development of said product. Modern personal computers, video games, and "Hummers" are examples of publicly subsidized consumer goods developed under government contract for supposed military use and then repackaged for domestic use at premium prices. This subsidized, or "Keynesian," model of capitalism was found to be more profitable than its "laissez-faire" predecessor because it represented a way of getting paid twice, first by the taxpayer and then by the consumer, who were, of course, one and the same.

Meanwhile the war, with millions of men "under arms" and not performing productive work, demonstrated the extent to which the public could exist simply as passive purchasers. While the GIs produced nothing (except perhaps death and disfigurement), the government subsidized all their needs. The problems of food, clothing, housing, sanitation, and recreation became the domain of massive corporations, newly consolidated for the war effort, and contracted by the government via the taxpayer.

Finally, the USA had displaced Great Britain as the foremost imperial power, outright occupying much of the globe with military bases. With territories, and the exotic goods that can be exploited from them, comes an inevitable need for moneyed markets.

All these developments led to the ruling class's reorganization of their commercial priorities and their profound redesignation of their serf/underling from his former role as "laborer" or "hayseed" to his new role as "buyer." Shopping would be his new pastime.

First, though, a radical transformation of the culture was needed to change the population from fairly self-sufficient farmers and craftspeople with a "Depression mentality" and "Christian work ethic" into perfectly efficient consumers.

This would require a conversion from the Christian doctrine of denial to a new capitalist religion of eating a lot.

This religion would be called "rock 'n' roll." While Christians had learned to do without, and based an entire ideology on it (to the extent that their clergy had no possessions and were actually celibate), rockers would defer no pleasure or desire, as expressed in the Black Flag song "Gimme Gimme Gimme."

While Christians were taught that sex was a disgusting sin and that dressing up was vanity, rock 'n' roll's very name was a euphemism for fornication, and special clothes were a prerequisite for membership.

—

Because rock never announced itself as a religion, the cults coexisted and actually still do. The ideologies, however, are so antagonistic that the facade of fraternity is difficult to maintain.

Despite their mutual hatred, there are uncanny similarities. Both cults are evangelical, tirelessly attempting to convert and then retain new "believers," without whose monetary contributions each dogma could not sustain its power. The individual vessels of indoctrination, whether priests or group/band members, are disposable and give their lives to serve the faith/ideology itself.

These people's missionary work (in rock parlance, "touring") aims to bring the entire earth under its yoke, with an institutionalized intolerance for other religious/musical forms.

Both are concerned with pedophilia, with the Church's being an outgrowth of a repressed sexuality and cyclical abuse, and rock 'n' roll's being a part of the capitalistic worship of newness. Rock songs are rife with lyrical references to very young girls as objects of desire: "Sweet Little Sixteen," "Only Sixteen," "Stray Cat Blues," "Jailbait," "She's Just 15," etc. While Christians idolize the virginal hymen, and therefore focus on deflowering boys, rockers are not so preoccupied, exalting little girls who are "bad" or "sluts," a.k.a. voracious consumers.

Like the priest with his "God," the rock group sermonizes about the eternal greatness of rock 'n' roll as singular faith and ideology; songs declare that "rock and roll can never die" and "Long Live Rock." "Roll Over Beethoven" and "Rock and Roll Music" express a hateful and colonial attitude toward other music forms that don't have the same commercial components.

In the feral sermon, the electric priest dispenses his version of this nasty "faith"—rock 'n' roll—as life-giving, soul-saving doctrine.

Besides announcing desire, the rock star also pays homage to the apostles who forged their faith from its blues origins, either Bo Diddley, Elvis Presley, or Ike Turner, depending on the received version of history. In addition to these brave "apostles" or originators, rock 'n' roll stars also ritualistically genuflect before their faith's progenitors, the "bluesmen" who preceded their form.

All groups, especially during the golden group era of the sixties, would humbly recite an Old Testament blues standard, in deference to these storied fabulons. Many groups dedicated themselves entirely to deciphering the hallowed scriptures of these holy men (e.g., Bluesbreakers et al.).

In the rock-as-religion analogy, these mythic blues figures would be the Old Testament Jewish prophets, such as Moses, David, and Saul. Indeed, it would be safe to say that blacks are the Jews of rock, with the few blacks passing through the magic portal from blues or "black music" to rock or "white music" being akin to the controversial "Jews for Jesus" sect.

In fact, rock's initial charisma stemmed from its ability to impart "blackness" upon the adherent. Similarly, Christianity was designed as a way for envious "goyim" to inherit the exclusive mantle of Jewishness, which theretofore had been a snooty bloodline, with rigid genetic gateways.

Jesus was the Jew who invited the resentful pagan outsiders to share in the splendor of self-righteous monotheism. (The Christian's Jew-envy extends in modern geopolitics to the invasions of Lebanon and Iraq, with their simulations of the Israeli occupation.)

After Jesus, anyone who "believed in Him" could effectively be a Jew: worshipping Jehovah, and entering the same heaven as Solomon, Abel, and Moses. By introducing a diluted pantheism in the form of "the Trinity" (and later, the Saints), Christians attracted pagans who were initially turned off by the dull prospect of having just one god.

Chuck Berry was rock's analogous Jesus, as he played a jump-blues with lyrics designed to appeal to white teenybop audiences. This was a tacit, Christlike invitation for ofays to "join the tribe."

Before his eventual stardom, clubgoers at his St. Louis residency would talk about the "black hillbilly." Through his teachings, Old Testament blues was merged with hillbilly music to spawn the new hybrid faith "rock 'n' roll."

At Berry's signal, the disciples Elvis Presley and Bill Haley appropriated blues slang, fashion, and dancing, allowing white children to partake safely of the forbidden world of black ritual.

In a segregated culture that subscribes even now to the myth of race and racial essentialism, this was a radical step. After Berry, black culture was attainable as long as one had the proper gear. (In the capitalist cult, as opposed to Christianity, belief was not enough but went in tandem with consumerism: ownership of sacred clothes and/or hairdos.) Just as ancient Jewish ancestry imparts an inscrutable validity on Christianity, so does rock's mysterious African genealogy.

Despite being supremacist doctrines, both faiths borrow their ancestors' oppressed "outsider" perspective from which they draw justification for triumphalist and voracious expansion. Christianity's entire identity is the self-righteous victimhood of "the crucifixion" and the "Stations of the Cross." All this self-pitying, despite the Crusades, the Inquisition, the Christian persecution of pagans, and the mass accumulation of wealth of the world's richest religion. The Vatican might be the most successful imperial power in history.

Similarly, rock 'n' roll is always sung in an outside voice, against an oppressive society that won't allow the acolytes to live as they wish. This is borrowed from a blues perspective, which expressed the suffering of the American underclass. This, despite rock's ubiquity and status as acme American music form, performed during halftime at the Super Bowl.

Appropriated by rockers, this voice of rebellion, alienation, and entitlement has become the national paradigm. It is the narrative of the culture. Everyone is an outsider (even the president), and everyone is proud of it.

As with the Jews with regard to the Christians, blacks were eventually resented by their rock offspring, who were self-conscious of their own mimicry and paranoid about their faith's derivative origins and inherited expression. Black musicians are almost entirely excluded from rock 'n' roll radio playlists with few exceptions (though cover versions of black artists' songs are common), and many adherents of later sectarian movements such as Southern rock, heavy metal, punk, goth, industrial, and even techno are proud of the "whiteness" of their respective genres, which in their imagination liberates them from their forerunners' formal debt to black artistic masters. The "Disco Sucks" movement was latently racist, as are many renowned superstar radio jocks who pander to chauvinist rock audiences.

In religion, anti-Semitic resentment manifested itself in genocidal policies that persisted in Europe for almost two thousand years. The Christians, having lifted their faith from Judaism, now desired to eradicate all traces of their plagiarism. Though culminating in the Nazi

"Holocaust," ghettos and mass murder of Jews were typical features of European life since the Christian ascendancy, especially during the Crusades and the Inquisition.

Is rock 'n' roll's resentment of its black progenitors a factor in the continued marginalization, economic repression, and police terror that haunt black America so long after Emancipation? Or is the continued marginalization of black people actually necessary for rock 'n' roll to retain any kind of mystic power, as the ancestors' suffering serves to grant the spiritual progeny (the rockers/capitalist heroes) a right to excess?

—

Rock 'n' roll and Christianity both have saints who achieve their status through total belief and subsequent martyrdom.

While Christian saints were killed by pagan infidels for refusing to repent faith in the fantastical idea of Christ's resurrection, the rock martyrs (Jim, Jimi, Janis, etc.) all died through a manic expo of the rock 'n' roll pleasure principle, taken to its extreme and nihilistic conclusion.

By killing themselves, they refute the Christian god and become their own god/master of destiny, the credo of capitalism and capitalism's ultimate metaphysical expressions—Satanism and Scientology.

The rock martyrs are ultimately admired for having "eaten too much," the folly of the great consumer. Acolytes strive to consume as much as these heroes did in their own drug binges, self-destructive homages to the idols of ingestion.

Nearly every sect that grew from rock 'n' roll was expressly interested in saving the medium's original mystic energy and promise from the perversions of later generations. This original promise was the feeling that first energized one to become an acolyte, a mix of sexual desperation, entitlement, and violent desire. Conversion stories about rock and particularly its most fanatic sect, "punk," eerily resemble born-again stories of being "saved."

Some groups are interested in broadening what they perceive as a limited early rock palate, determined to free the medium from what they see as a stultifying orthodoxy. These people, known as "prog rockers," attempt to fuse jazz (which in an analogical sense could be seen as Buddhism) with rock 'n' roll so as to make rock richer and more expansive. This impulse is echoed in the theosophical hippie cults that flourished in the seventies.

Usually, though, the impulse is to purify the perverted form, as with the Christian Reformation.

In Christianity, the Reformation was an outgrowth of popular resentment toward Church corruption, fomented and financed by the new slave-trading imperialist class (called the bourgeoisie) who desired to break the domination of the Catholic Church and the royalty and ascend to power themselves. The struggle between the two ideologies—the bourgeois "Protestants" and royalist Catholics—resulted in especially cruel wars that lasted two centuries, completely transforming Europe.

During and after the Reformation, countless Protestant sects were spawned that rejected the wealth and worldliness of the Vatican and adhered to Christ's original tenets of poverty, as they were thought to have been taught by a sort of protocommunard Jesus.

The Reformation in rock would be "punk," which in turn spawned a thousand sects, each one announcing its claim as the bearer of the true flame.

Punk, too, was an outgrowth of popular resentment about the course rock 'n' roll, with its hypocrite populist rhetoric, had taken. This movement, like Protestantism, was alternately despised and bankrolled by the ruling class according to their various purposes. From punk came hardcore, goth, grind, speed and black metal, straight edge, indie pop, etc., as well as the revival and/or popularization of ska, rockabilly, garage, industrial, and noise music.

Punk, the great reformation of rock, had been highly anticipated in the years that preceded its appearance. It was, in fact, an inevitable convulsion since a rebel stance was intrinsic to the rock 'n' roll matrix.

Rebellion "for its own sake" as ideology perfectly served an ever-transformative market with its fashion waves that receded to and fro. Because punk was a mass revolt against its parent form, some of its sectarian developments actually slightly resembled rock's nemesis, Christianity, with an emphasis on moderation, self-flagellation, or denial.

These would be the "crust," "anarchist," and "straight edge" cult variants. Work cults like indie rock resembled Seventh-day Adventists, garage and rockabilly purists resembled the Amish (for whom history has stopped at a certain moment), while industrialists were like the medieval flagellants, though for them the flesh was the object of worship and not simply an unfortunate barrier between themselves and the pure soul. Heavy metal people, being polygamist, arcane, and simultaneously conservative, resemble Mormons.

Though some of these sects seem to rebuke capitalism, they are still tied to a market system, helming record companies that ultimately infuse the market system and whet the consumer's appetite.

Despite aberrant, crypto-Judaic impulses, punk overwhelmingly reignited rock's original mission, which had been fading with the long careers of the seventies' rock artists. Punk, as an "avant-garde" movement, stoked an obsession with newness and trendiness that was vital to a healthy market, and helped to retire the careers of many "artists" whose longevity belied the rock industry's planned-obsolescence theology. Rock had to appear new and not institutionalized, as it had become. Especially because it was being threatened by another music-based capitalist cult: *hip hop.*

A newer, leaner, more accessible, and slightly less Byzantine faith, hip hop is to rock 'n' roll as Islam is to Christianity, and is even more nakedly prostrate to their common deity: money.

Hip hop abandons the pretenses of artistry that have stymied rock's full potential as marketing force and ultimate capitalist mouthpiece, a fact underlined long ago by Run-DMC's smash hit "My Adidas." Though Carl Perkins declared his love for "Blue Suede Shoes," he never cited a brand name.

Just as Islam takes affront at Christianity's "pagan" Trinity, hip hop is a less diluted music style than rock, as it lacks the same white/country or "hillbilly" influences. Islam's originators, the Arabs, envision themselves as descendants of a Jewish prophet named Ishmael, who was "cast out" by Abraham. He traveled south from the Holy Land to found the tribes that would later conquer the Middle East and North Africa under Mohammed.

Hip hop shares the same genesis as rock (Old Testament "talking blues"), but is also derivative of Jamaican music called "dance hall." Though fractured by schisms (the East-West feud could be a parallel to the Shiite/Sunni split), "rap" is growing exponentially as rock and its various offspring (punk, et al.) shrink, cursed by the paradox of its own rhetoric.

Rock 'n' roll has been revealed as fatally

fuddy-duddy by the standards of its own capitalist matrix, whereby any stone that stops
rolling, even for a moment, is commercially
deceased. Meanwhile, hip hop has absolutely
no regard for the extended "careers" of its "artists." In this way, hip hop is impervious, where
rock, with its old-fashioned pretense of artistic
integrity, is endangered.

Even more fatal than hip hop to rock's future as primary ideological conduit, though, is
the rock 'n' roll fan's own studied disinterest
in the medium: as with Christianity, a lack of
belief in itself has transferred to lack of faith of
the followers in its own dogma.

While rock as religion once had a fanatic
base of closed-minded zealots (parallel to
Christianity in its heyday), it now typically en-
counters a cynical and half-interested constit-
uency. Instead of the purists who once argued
for rock's primacy against any and all competing forms, today's teenybopper gives credence
to multifarious musical styles. These so-called
enthusiasts are more akin to the aforementioned prog rocker than to one of Bill Haley's

famous hellcats, who tore up the theater seats of his early performances.

Yes, nowadays rock 'n' roll fans are open-minded and collect all kinds of genres of music. They no longer fetishize the records they buy but download them from the Internet, seeing them as disposable fluff to be discarded after a single listen. Rock shows no longer have body-trampling fans, and instead are lousy with disinterested spectators.

These fans resemble the compulsory attendees of Methodist churches across America, who show up out of some guilt or social compunction but display no ardor for their cause. The music is almost entirely stripped of meaning, and lacks the impassioned intent of the old standards: "Dancing in the Street," "All You Need Is Love," "Clash City Rockers," and "Mama Weer All Crazee Now" are replaced with a drone and a mumble because there is no point to make.

This, because capitalism is no longer an ideology with competitors. Socialism is destroyed and the global market economy/imperialism is like the air we breathe—not a point for debate but an inescapable fact.

Since rock was, in subterfuge, capitalism's secret exponent, in victory it no longer has a mission. It is replaced by hip hop, which, instead of trumpeting the ideology, focuses on hyping and promulgating particular luxury products.

While Christianity's message of denial was destroyed by the consumer society's enforcement of desire, which decimated its once-mighty congregations, rock 'n' roll's dogma simply became redundant, resulting in a similar abandonment.

Despite its ever-transformative, hyperprotean nature, it was overtaken and destroyed by the accelerated market forces it originally announced, like the rabbi with his golem. Though ideologically opposed, rock 'n' roll and Christianity share yet another thing: the same assassin.

6

THE RESPONSIBLE USE
OF ROCK 'N' ROLL

... I considered Hitler a complete masochist
possessed by the idea of provoking a war in
order to lose it heroically.

SALVADOR DALÍ

On discussing anything nowadays, from the
vulgar and mundane to rarefied art or fine
wine, the famous dictator Adolf Hitler will
invariably be invoked.

In fact, no contemporary film, book, magazine essay, or anonymous public bathroom
encounter is really complete without the drop-
ping of his famous name. This is supposedly
because he is such a handy and unparalleled
embodiment of absolute evil, useful for the
simplistic reductions so common in the airy
banter of ball life. But his staying power as star
of modern chitchat is really because his story

illuminates the unacknowledged role of the artist in shaping destiny.

His story is one that everyone knows. The crazed dictator who tried to take over the earth, but who was halted because his ambition was too great and his heart was too small. Yet for a man supposedly driven to conquer the world and establish a "thousand-year Reich," Adolf Hitler exhibited very peculiar behavior.

He systematically alienated influential and high-ranking sympathizers in the US and Britain (Henry Ford, William Randolph Hearst, Joe Kennedy, John Rockefeller, Andrew Mellon, Allen Dulles, the list goes on)—men who didn't influence government policy but rather set it. Burning these strategic bridges, Hitler challenged the whole of the industrial world, including the US, though the nation was bloated with endless pustules of men, money, and munitions. He also ordered, in a holy war against communism, the historically suicidal invasion of Russia, despite the disasters of Charles XII and Napoleon looming as cautionary tales. Such actions make clear that Hitler's ambition was not politics, but immolation.

For him, the script to this final act, the invasion of Russia, unfolded with storybook perfection. After tremendous success, the Nazi rampage was halted in the snow of Stalingrad, and the slaughter reversed. The Red Army, the verminous inverse composite of his own beloved racially pure stormtroopers, overran Germany and its various Eastern allies. Surrounded by Bolshevik *untermensch* in a Berlin bunker, Hitler apparently managed to bite into a cyanide capsule whilst simultaneously firing a Luger into his mouth. He did so while draped in the arms of his freshly poisoned lover.

Like Wagner's heroes Siegfried and Tristan, Hitler's struggle had been gloriously futile, an epic to be recounted as myth. As a great fan of opera, suicide was almost certainly a highly cherished moment in a life characterized by unlikely and daring triumphs.

Hitler's story, though, is more than a

titillating morsel to recount for delight. It demonstrates that an examination of a leader's/culture's most beloved art can yield the destiny of that nation and people. That the popular expression of the culture is actually the narrative that determines its overarching historical course. To wit: as an opera enthusiast, Hitler had to lead Germany to a tragic Wagnerian calamity.

The ramifications regarding the responsibility of the use of "art" are profound. We could conclude, for example, that the American defeat in Vietnam was entailed by the tragi-poetic aesthetic of The Doors, Dylan, and Hendrix, who had led the culture on a teeny-bacchanalian death trip. And that the artist who works in the paradigmatic form of his or her time holds the key to their culture, nation, and collective destiny. If the leaders are hip to this fact, it would explain the government's overweening interest in the content of art, and particularly film, which is the most pervasive and influential medium.

Of course, Hitler was no mere opera fan:

his participation with, and sponsorship by, various ultra-right-wing occult and esoteric neo-Gnostic groups such as the Thule Society and the Bavarian Illuminati are well known.

Though Hitler already possessed the "Spear of Destiny," his archaeologists were saddled with exploration of theoretical lands like Hyperborea and the excavation of holy Christian relics in places like Rennes-le-Château.

But, opposed to these distractions, Wagner was a spirit who was central to the ideals of the Third Reich. German opera eclipsed Hitler's metaphysical mentors who were steeped in the Orientalism of Gurdjieff, Blavatsky, Zen, and the Vedas (influencing the Nazi appropriation of the swastika). Wagner was Hitler's guiding light.

Adolf Hitler credited a stirring performance of the Wagner opera *Rienzi* as the epiphanic moment that propelled him to seek political office. Once in power, Hitler said, "Whoever wants to understand National Socialist Germany must know Wagner"; "With the exception of Richard Wagner, I have no forerunner"; and "Out of *Parsifal*, I make a religion."

Not simply a composer of operas, Wagner was a German national hero in the late nineteenth century. An outspoken Jew-hater and cultural critic, he expounded influentially on the nature of Teutonic art. His race hatred was an outgrowth of that era's eugenic craze and the nineteenth-century aberration called nationalism. Inevitably, the Jew is displaced in this milieu as the "other." A mystic firebrand, Hitler insisted that "all Jews should be burned at a performance of *Nathan the Wise*," and that the only redemption for the tribe was "Ahasverus"—total destruction.

———

Wagner blamed Hebrew-inspired Christian guilt for Germany's inability to achieve its place as entitled ruler among nations, a claim later echoed by Hitler, who said, "Conscience is a Jewish invention, it is a blemish like circumcision." Hitler was enthralled with Wagner, who had been jingoistic, anti-Semitic, and cryptopagan, and Wagner's music apparently served as the death-camp soundtrack to the "Final Solution."

Though raised as a Roman Catholic and working in collusion with the Vatican until the end of his life, Hitler's state version of Christianity was interbred with pagan and nationalist rituals inspired by Wagner's Nordic-Gnostic hybrid and its attempt to cleanse the Church of its Jewish root. Both men were influenced by the *völkisch* philosophy of Guido Von List, the Austro-German author of *The Secret of the Runes* and proponent of Odinism. Nazi ideology was appropriately mystical, driven by the notion of the *Volk,* German destiny, and a special warrior/priest class (the SS) in heroic conflict with state-appointed monsters, such as Bolsheviks, Gypsies, etc., the political manifestation of the metaphorical dwarves and dragons featured on Wagner's Bayreuth opera house stage.

This SS was modeled on the medieval order of Teutonic Knights, the German version of the Knights Templar, who, instead of trying for the Holy Land, colonized the pagan Baltic states and northern Russia during Crusades in the twelfth and thirteenth centuries.

German imperial strategy during the Third Reich was to forgo the far-flung colonial possessions that typified the British/French paradigm and instead expand eastward à la these knights of yore in a strategy reminiscent of the United States' "Manifest Destiny." This would create Lebensraum in an enormous Grossdeutschland.

This explains the inclusion of Slavs as *untermensch* in Nazi eugenics theory, and the extermination of Russians during the German invasion along with Jews and Gypsies. As always, ideology is contrived to underwrite guilt and expedite policy. The SS were to be the feudal lords who would rule the surviving Slavs during German settlement. Of course, Wagner's *Parsifal* features the famous Templar Order who guard the Holy Grail.

The Berlin Opera was commissioned to design SS officer uniforms, to give them an appropriately sharp and menacing look. The Nazis were an aesthetic cult, after all, as exemplified by Leni Riefenstahl's films, Speer's *Cathedral of Light,* and the rally at Nuremberg. But the underlying aesthetic narrative for Nazi Germany was opera, particularly the unremittingly tragic works of Richard Wagner.

Each regime has an aesthetic program through which it propagates its ideology. Art in the Soviet Union had been derailed in the early thirties from an avant-garde "constructivism" under Lenin to a populist and anti-intellectual form called "social realism" under Stalin. Pictures and films of this genre propagated a heroic vision of revolutionary proletarian life in a way that could be understood and appreciated by the imagined lumpen masses. "Now art is for everyone" was the official explanation.

The philistine neutering of the revolution's ambitious and visionary artistic program can be blamed, more than any other factor, for the eventual destruction of Soviet communism at the hands of American imperialist bankers in the late twentieth century. Instead of Maya-kovsky's and Rodchenko's daring innovations, the vogue was for sun-dappled scenes and portraits of field hands. Still, despite stultify-ing aesthetic guidelines, some extraordinary artists prevailed, such as El Lissitzky and film-maker Sergei Eisenstein.

In 1938, the Soviets commissioned an im-portant film by Eisenstein which determined their distinct narrative for the inevitable col-lision with their militarized German neme-sis. Called *Alexander Nevsky*, the film took place in the Middle Ages and was based on the exploits of the Russian prince Alexander Nevsky, who defeated the Teutonic knights as they raped and burned through Russia in one of the many Eastern Crusades that served as pretext for Templar/German colonization.

The story begins with the German knights and their priestly entourage burning babies and pillaging cities—*as was exactly the case in the war three years later.*

The Germans are at first fantastically suc-cessful but are eventually led onto the ice lake by the wily Alexander in an uncanny prophecy of the Stalingrad disaster.

Their heavy armor proves their undoing and, just as the mechanized blitzkrieg was undone by the Russian winter, the Teutonic knights fall to their watery death in the frozen lake.

The art forms that are used as propaganda by the rival powers are of course instructive, as they illuminate perfectly the respective ideologies at play. For the communists, the mythic Nazi approach is replaced by a historic and filmed "scientific" one. Opera had been the soundtrack to imperial conquest, its inception actually coinciding with the advent of the Western European imperial age. Wagner was one of the last serious opera composers, just as Nazi Germany seemed to be the last example of the old style of empire building, and his work is also considered the acme of the genre in terms of seriousness and difficulty.

Eisenstein, meanwhile, was on the front line of innovation in film, the medium Lenin called the "most important of the arts." His stylized photography and jump cuts revolutionized movies and are still used as reference today. He had imagined himself as near to a "pure cinematography" that was "genetically ideological," and he dreamed of making a filmic version of Marx's *Das Kapital*.

—

The soundtrack for *Nevsky* was by Prokofiev, a composer who had gained renown for his modernist musical tracts and whom the Western musical establishment had denounced as an agent of Bolshevism. Could these two have known, when commissioned to create this film, that they were filming and editing their nation's destiny? Or did the Nazis have an inner sense that for them—mired in their operatic death trip—defeat in the conflict was all but assured?

Alexander Nevsky was called a "plasto-cinematographic symphony" because it was, like opera, entirely ersatz, stylized, and obsessively premeditated. Eisenstein was actually interested in realizing opera's goal, "the synthesis of all arts," but in film. In fact, he said that *Battleship Potemkin,* his early masterpiece, was "built up in accordance with the laws of austere composition of tragedy in its traditional five-act form." But *Nevsky,* made in the face of the actual Nazi menace, was created as a propaganda film to stir the people's hearts to action and precluded any doomed ending.

—

The underlying artistic narrative was the crux; the triumphalist nature of the Soviet propaganda contrasted with the heroic doomed tragedy of German opera. As the armies clashed, the end was predetermined, though it would cost millions of lives and horrible suffering. Hitler was a romantic intent on death and Stalin a realist bent on survival.

This revelation illuminates much, particularly the state sponsorship for all manners of film coming from Hollywood now.

While the US Army and Navy subsidize

movies such as *The Sum of All Fears* almost entirely, they insist on cursory scrubbing of the scripts, ensuring not only triumphalist endings, but the heroic behavior of men in American uniform. The rulers in Washington seem aware of the importance of the invisible hand of art in determining the destiny of the nation. Though the denigration and parody of "the artist" (excepting those beset by fantastic success) is de rigueur in the culture, we see that his or her power is actually secretly resented and admired as being key to predestination.

This reveals much more, though, than the simple subsidization of *Windtalkers, Extreme Ops, The Recruit,* etc. It is a telling exposé of the culture's discomfort with the European tradition of "high art" and particularly of tragedy. While the Old World still cultivates the traditions of painting, poetry, and dance, the United States of America and its spiritual godfather Great Britain have implemented an institutionalized disregard for these forms. In these Protestant neocolonial mercantile capitals, only "art" which is commercially viable and populist is a respectable pursuit, à la rock 'n' roll music, movies, and commercial or "pop" art.

The Beatles, Scorsese, and Warhol are exalted while the old forms of bourgeois culture such as poetry, painting, symphony, etc. (the "high arts"), are despised as effete and boring. This actually echoes the kibosh Stalin put on "elitist" art forms in his institutionalization of social realism. This is no whim of culture, but an officially enforced arbitration designed to maintain an uncomplicated triumphalist narrative as the national expression.

England led the way in this philistinism, replying to Europe's tragic operatic canon with the fluff of Gilbert and Sullivan, and to the plays of Strindberg and Ibsen with Oscar Wilde. The US followed suit with Charlie Chaplin and Rodgers and Hart. Nietzsche had postulated that in art there was a "Dionysian" urge for self-immolation and passion that intruded on the "Apollonian" urge for symmetry, construction, and conquest, the union of the two finding its expression in the medium "tragedy."

To Nietzsche, it was the apex of beauty, this tragic urge that came to characterize "high art." After his death, with his texts politically perverted by party members, Nietzsche's works became Nazi staples. Nietzsche's first book, *The Birth of Tragedy,* is an homage to Wagner's tragic operas. This Dionysian, passionate, suicidal urge is certainly present in the rock 'n' roll genre, with its death cult (Hendrix, Morrison, Cobain), and in film, which is preoccupied almost exclusively with murder and violence, but the framing narrative itself is triumphalist, on the radio with "freedom rock" and the "pop" format, and especially in film with the ubiquitous "Hollywood ending."

This narrative in the official forms of expression is enforced maniacally, for once the Dionysian takes hold, the cultural arbiters understand that it spells the end of the empire. The European disinclination toward war points to the defeatism that inevitably follows when a culture embraces "high art" and ascribes nuanced, existential, or tragic conclusions to its artworks. Art with this trajectory simultaneously humanizes victimhood in a manner that ultimately condemns the mass murder of imperialism. It also programs in its adherents an unconscious desire for noble defeat and immolation.

The American imperial high command sees the writing on the wall. If Sylvester Stallone dies, the empire crumbles. Indeed, "Rocky" lost the big fight only in the first film—a product of the pacifist, war-hating seventies. Since then, he has smashed the Russians, reinvaded Vietnam, and so forth, and the American fascists' fortunes have risen with him. The brief post–golden age glimmer for provocative auteur cinema in the US was the 1970s: a low point for jingoism, with America losing in Angola, Laos, Nicaragua, and Vietnam. Then *Star Wars* and George Lucas ushered in Ronald Reagan and the revitalized military state.

Wagner's heyday came on the heels of the Franco-Prussian War of 1870, the final great military victory for Germany. After his tragic narrative was introduced, all of Deutschland's wars were defeats, though the Teutonic armies had no equal. Finally, through this strange transposition, he murdered his biggest fan. Great, nuanced art brings beauty but also doom, the overlords understand.

The ruling class must therefore studiously maintain a life without appreciation for anything beyond money, baubles, gadgets, power, and military hardware: a philistine's existence which has transformed our world into the strip mall we inhabit. Their fear of "art" is palpable, though they use it, especially cinema and rock 'n' roll, to subjugate the world to an American economic hegemony.

While cinema is the state's favorite tool for global indoctrination, because of the budgetary excesses that make it so easy to pervert through subsidization, rock 'n' roll is a more unwieldy weapon. Cheap enough to be made by anyone, its content is less easily determined because it doesn't require government or industry handouts.

This rock 'n' roll has so far been mostly constrained by strict aesthetic parameters that are critically enforced. In its current conservative manifestation, it has been a most effective instrument for subjugating foreign markets and ideologies, but as an official expression of the culture, it can and must be subverted and utilized in a way that truly best serves the world—to bring destruction to the war machine, to crush the reactionaries, and to slaughter the high command as Wagner did, unwittingly, from his grave.

This awesome power and responsibility, rock 'n' rollers, lies with you.

Dylan As Prometheus

7

EAT THE ROCUMENT

Folk music is a bunch of fat people.
BOB DYLAN, 1966

Because rock 'n' roll is, in subterfuge, a religion of sorts, and also a covert cultural narrative, its constructed mythology is central to its power and also a key to understanding its intended use.

Of all the sixties rock 'n' roll legends and myths, the fable of Dylan going electric is the most significant.

The story goes, of course, that he bucked the closed-minded folk establishment at the 1965 Newport Folk Festival by plugging in his guitar and rocking out. The purists in the crowd booed and Pete Seeger supposedly tried to chop the electric cable with an ax to cut the power.

Dylan then broke with the folk movement,

forsaking its hypocrisy, and kick-started "folk-rock."

This legend has been institutionalized by the culture industry. It announces a mythic heroism not only for the protagonist in his epic battle against the homely folk-Stalinist bogeymen but also for the industry itself, in its noble struggle against independent/provincial music "scenes" and the unfair imposition of aesthetic restrictions on art and business.

Rock 'n' roll, as the paradigmatic liberal art form, must be given free rein to swallow its competitors through co-optation and inclusion. The industry's marginalization of folkies as closed-minded bigots serves them well in their typical propagation of a fantasy narrative from which to suspend their catalogue of products. A catalogue through which one may purchase his or her very own piece of rebellion: by buying electric Dylan, one buys against fuddy-duddy doctrinaire culture clerics.

The official historic account serves to sell Columbia-brand record product of course, but also and much more importantly constant transformation as an intrinsic aspect of music and all art. The fable "Dylan Goes Electric" is history in the service of commerce, and was so convincingly sold that it served the industry's aim to demolish independent and political music for years afterward.

In 1965, Dylan was the future embodied for the folk-revival movement, the politicized and independent music phenomenon that had started during the fifties in reaction to the restructuring of American life into McCarthyism, consumerism, and automobile-based suburban conformity.

The folk movement, though now dismissed as square, parochial, and irrelevant, was the prototype for the media version of the sixties, with the same Orientalism, sexual freedom, drugs, and political activism which typified that more ballyhooed later era. (The hippie "sixties," as they are referred to, really occurred between 1966 and 1975.)

Indeed, the folkies and their "beatnik" counterparts wrote the script for the "hippies," whom they would birth. As opposed to their more commerce-minded and me-dia-savvy offspring, however, the movers in the folk movement weren't particularly hung up on songwriting or even originality, since individualism was bourgeois; they were more interested in the archaeology of poor people's music of all types. Their aims were socialistic and their great white father was the Roos-evelt-era song collector Alan Lomax, who had scoured America for undocumented music forms during the New Deal. That was in the thirties, when nationalist and racialist move-ments were all the rage in Europe (especially in Germany, England, and Italy), and envi-ous Americans needed evidence of a distinct American culture and heritage.

Lomax famously trolled through the South, taping miners, farmers, and prisoners in search of an "authentic American voice." His employer was the government, his aims propagandistic: the construction of a national identity out of the tangled murky weirdness of the backwoods.

Lomax found it in spades, with blues, gospel, protest songs, work songs, and ballads, plus he "discovered" Woody Guthrie and Huddie "Lead Belly" Ledbetter (ironic that nationalist types like Hitler were ultimately responsible for the scholarly significance placed on blues and folk music, previously ignored by academics). The "folkniks," as they were called (-*nik* being a Russian suffix implying Red/communist), saw the utilization of this "folk" or people's art as a powerful weapon in their struggle against the encroaching industrialization of their lives. The writing was on the wall, with America already ballooning full bore into the Cold War/arms race/foreign intervention/fast-food-mongering mode, which is now just business as usual.

The folk scene developed around song collectors who would play these old songs at coffeehouses in universities and cities across America. They developed a national community of small record labels and mimeographed magazines which resembled the hardcore punk phenomenon of the 1980s (itself spawned by the McCarthyesque Reagan administration).

This music network expounded a very distinct political philosophy, aligned with the civil rights movement, nuclear disarmament, etc. As the Communist Party had recently been destroyed by the FBI, the folkniks (as fellow travelers) took up many of its causes—such as "Negro" rights, women's rights, workers' rights—that no longer had an organized champion. Folk even featured on-the-run pinkos like Seeger himself, who had been jailed for a year by HUAC during the communist witch hunt.

Labels like Vanguard and Moe Asch's Folkways issued modern renditions of old songs, always done acoustically and with deference to the tradition in which they had historically been sung. (Electric music was considered teenybop music, cranked out by a music factory for the exclusive purpose of making money. The contemporaries in rock 'n' pop were Dion, Fabian, Paul Anka, and the surf and doo-wop groups.)

Bob Dylan started in this traditionalist vein too. When he recorded his first album for Columbia (*Bob Dylan*, 1961), he performed only one song he had actually written, "Song to Woody," for the man (Woody Guthrie) whose style he had appropriated. The other tunes were coffeehouse standards that his contemporaries were also playing.

As he continued working, however, he acquired a manager, called Albert Grossman, who wasn't constrained by the niceties of the folk scene.

Grossman saw that the money in music was in publishing, and he recognized Dylan's protean songwriting capabilities. He encouraged Dylan's writing, even setting him up an office at the Brill Building (an institution despised by folkniks), and ordered his other managed acts (most notably Peter, Paul and Mary) to perform Dylan's songs, thereby breaking him to audiences that would have found his voice undesirable. Every night at their sold-out concerts, before singing "Blowin' in the Wind," Peter, Paul and Mary were induced to announce that it had been written by "the most important young songwriter in America today, Bob Dylan."

Grossman also nurtured in him a bourgeois disdain for the well-meaning folkies. The folk scene could be characterized as "maternal," guided by a caregiving, familial ethos, and Dylan was fed and housed by many of the scene "mamas" when he first arrived in NYC, posing as a hobo.

Each year the great folk event was the curated outdoor festival at Newport, where the cream of the scene would play. Dylan was launched at the Newport Folk Festival like a debutante, with great pomp and circumstance, by Joan Baez, who was the reigning queen of folk.

He was immediately a great hit. Dylan could write anthems as well as love songs, and he emerged as a distinctive singer and stage personality as well. His palette included the protest song and the surreal, drug-inspired poetry of the beats and their masters, the French symbolists.

For a time, Dylan was content with his new kingdom, and he treated his subjects with charm and deference. But in 1964, when he first heard The Beatles on the radio, he recognized the future: his alpha male instincts took over and he vowed not to be left behind.

With The Beatles, folk music had met its biggest potential threat, bigger than the blacklist, lack of airplay, or poor distribution for independent records. For The Beatles were a romantic template for rock 'n' roll, not the Mafia-owned, payola-driven, wax-haired Phil Spectorites of the past. They were sure to attract a sizable piece of the middle-class college kids who were folk music's usual audience. They were witty and sharp, had presidential access to the media, and made the folkies look moralistic and self-serious. To top it all off, they utilized electricity.

The folk establishment took solace, though, in the fact that, in their arsenal, they held a trump card: Dylan. Widely respected, he was both politically righteous and absolutely cool. He hung out with Ginsberg and refused to perform on TV when he couldn't do his incendiary "Talkin' John Birch Paranoid Blues." He spoke in riddles and wrote psychedelic verse on his record sleeves. However popular and young these English carpetbaggers were, none were as daunting or complex as the prolific and poetic man from Hibbing, their very own folk Rimbaud.

Of course, his team didn't know that he, like America, was under The Beatles' spell. For The Beatles' spell was in fact the spell of the group, the group of men and the particular way they communicated obliquely through inference and humor. Folk was, with all its communistic rhetoric, the pageant of the plainspoken man or woman, attempting as it did to popularize socialist politics through traditional song forms. Socialism could be characterized as a "maternal" ideology, with its emphasis on caregiving and nurturing its subjects' needs. Though there was a masculine wanderers' aesthetic in folk (the "ramblin' hobo"), the prevalent ideology was communal/familial.

Dylan himself was a lothario and a misogynist, and he recognized in The Beatles a way to escape the maternal and culpable world he found himself in. He, like many American men, envied their manly cluster, which deflected criticism and feminine control. The Beatles of course were beyond lady killing, being more akin to Bhopal eunuchs: they made women redundant, appropriating their effeminate hairdos and jewelry, and singing in pretty harmonies that outshone even Baez.

Theirs was the image that set the woman-hating sixties in motion, when the establishment would promulgate the ideal of femininity as Twiggy/Pattie Boyd: a silent and childlike sex kitten. The Beatles' announcement was this: that in the postwar prosperity, men would be relieved of the responsibilities that had burdened their fathers: the mantle of family and jobs and going to war. From now on, the man would behave like a teenager.

This message would be codified with the hippies, who set about on a program of adolescent ribaldry, bourgeois excess, and narcissistic street theater. They would flip the script of the folkies, utilizing their aesthetic for an absolutely self-centered—as opposed to communal—ideology. This would culminate in the modern individualist era, initially referred to as "the me generation."

Dylan's announcement of betrayal was at first coded, and appeared immediately after his Beatles epiphany. The record *Another Side of Bob Dylan* (1964) was explicitly apolitical except for those songs that expressed disenchantment with the program of the folk cult ("It Ain't Me Babe," "My Back Pages," "It's All Over Now, Baby Blue").

These cryptic and poetic statements slipped by his elders, though: a clean break would have to be made for Dylan to really shake his old crowd and run with the sexy and glamorous capitalist set.

Electric music was not altogether disdained by the folkies but its use to them represented market forces; the transformative nature of art, which we take for granted, is really a requirement of consumerism. Innovation for its own sake is the artistic version of planned obsolescence. The Beatles were pioneers in this hypercapitalist shape-shifting which has now become a rote exercise for anyone trying for a career longer than a single album.

The folk scene's focus on traditional music was a response to this idea. The coffeehouse scene was also based around community, sing-alongs, lyrical content, and intimacy—all aspects that would be destroyed by the introduction of electricity. Thus, when Dylan subsequently went electric at Newport with a very loud group, it was considered a middle finger to the tenets of the scene that had championed and raised him: a disavowal of a highly interactive milieu.

No one wants to be on the wrong side of history, so you would never find an admitted participant in the fabled booing at Newport, but the phenomenon wasn't isolated to that concert. Booing followed Dylan and the Band around the world to every hall they played. To modern sensibilities, it strikes one as a very strange reaction. In *Eat the Document,* the D.A. Pennebaker film of Dylan's electric tour, the crowd's disapproval seems perverse and bizarre.

This is because we are divorced from the context. What Dylan's audience decried was not the music, but the loss of an entire way of life: the coffeehouses, hootenannies, political fanzines, and music as message. It was a political problem, not merely rooted in aesthetics. Because, as they intuitively sensed, Dylan's gesture broke the back of the movement and it withered away, never to recover.

Dylan's rebellion was in fact *defection,* an embrace of capitalism and a rebuke of crypto-Commie ideology masquerading as a musical movement.

Like other high-profile defectors in the Cold War, Dylan was sure to be feted by the establishment with gushing and accolades. His seduction was a coup, and he became a war trophy, a big-game kill to be hung in public view.

Dylan wrote the folk movement's epitaph himself, with what could also be considered a kind of hex/curse, in an ominous interview for *Playboy* magazine: ". . . folk music is a word I can't use. Folk music is a bunch of fat people.

I have to think of all this as traditional music. Traditional music is based on hexagrams. It comes about from legends, Bibles, plagues, and it revolves around vegetables and death. There's nobody that's going to kill traditional music. All these songs about roses growing out of people's brains and lovers who are really geese and swans that turn into angels—they're not going to die. It's all those paranoid people who think that someone's going to come and take away their toilet paper—they're going to die. Songs like 'Which Side Are You On?' and 'I Love You, Porgy'—they're not folk music songs: they're political songs. They're already dead."

The folk movement was so completely wrecked by Dylan's verbal assaults in interviews and by the music establishment's relentless framing of history that the entire folk ideology seems incomprehensible now, as inscrutable as Prussian dueling scars or Aztec sacrifice.

—

The hippies merged the salable aspects of the folk movement with California surf culture and transformed them into a highly marketable self-centered "lifestyle," which lost any claim to its formerly radical character. Folk's protagonists took their place alongside the losers in the history book who are reduced to idiotic caricature, stripped of a voice and personified by their biggest flop.

As with any commercial stepchild, folk's former adherents don't even remember themselves as such. They reminisce along with the Time Life nostalgia series about Woodstock or miniskirts or whatever is officially designated as important and memory worthy. When one's personal history is systematically omitted from public records, one loses the sense of having lived at all.

One longs to share a collective experience with one's peers. An inevitable absorption of the official narrative takes root. The eyewitness to history slowly becomes an eyewitness to the version replayed on television and film:

the official history. Finally, when they are asked about seeing Mimi Farina they can only recall The Beatles on *Ed Sullivan* or their first hit of acid: facile clichés and marketing campaigns which are trumpeted as epochal events. They have a choice: accept the myth and be considered a by-product of a fantastical, epic era or be an incomprehensible old bore.

Mind-control/brainwashing techniques are all based on repetition of ideas in a completely nonreflexive atmosphere such as boot camp or television. Modern history's function is to reify the paradigmatic ideological systems by placing them in a fantasy framework. By erasing folk through omission, the movement's social mission is also erased, replaced by the frattish bourgeois antics of the Yippies and their peers the "Motherfuckers," etc.

Dylan's career of course flourished, including his folk period, redeemed by his timely conversion. The Newport debacle became his standard commercial strategy, to disappoint the faithful in whatever form they took, so as to always appear avant-garde.

"Dylan Goes Electric" was—and as myth, still is—another proxy struggle of market forces against latent communist egalitarianism.

8

TIME AS MONEY

Since so much of the discussion regarding cultural control thus far has centered around music, we must now confront a timely question:

What is music?

Music is discussed in terms of notes and tones, songs and chords. But the most essential ingredient to music is actually *time*.

While what is called music can include any array of sounds and nonsounds, all of it, every genre, including John Cage's famous silent composition, relies on time to convey its purpose.

Time, meanwhile, is held in such high regard as to be considered equal to or interchangeable with money, promulgated by the phrase "time is money," which in turn is the central pursuit of the culture. Time is therefore a commodity, something that must be controlled by financiers and speculators, like oil and real estate. A central basis for the economy and the underlying obsession of the modern world, industrial innovation is focused mostly on "saving time" or contracting the moments it takes to normally perform a task.

Time = money is an economic equation derived from the scholarship that if life is the pursuit of money (life = money) and time is the primary aspect of life (life = time), then necessarily time = money. In an inevitable adjunct, the essential time component of music makes it the preeminent modern art form. Because music requires a commitment of time from the listener, it is now considered precious in a way other art forms are not. As opposed to painting and other static forms, one cannot experience music at one's convenience, diverting one's attention when one wishes. One must listen to music in its time-specific entirety. While, according to statistics, an American tourist can race through the Louvre Museum in nine minutes and forty-six seconds, absorbing thousands of nuanced artworks with each moment, it takes forty-one minutes and fifty-seven seconds to listen to the *Enantiodromia* album by Azita in its entirety.

This amount of time can't be bisected or sped up in any way while still maintaining the unmarred integrity of the piece. Similarly, if one hasn't spent the whole 2:23 it takes to hear Wilson Pickett's "Land of a Thousand Dances," one has not really listened to, or "heard," that particular song.

Meanwhile, a single glance at the *Mona Lisa* constitutes it having been "seen" by the viewer. The viewer commands the time in this scenario, while with music it's the opposite: the medium controls or determines the experience, whether live or canned.

Thereby, borne of the spectator's ability to deflect his own eyes from Mona Lisa's famous gaze comes the exalted privilege of amplified, modulated sound (along with the similarly time-based/blessed medium of film) in modernity.

Because time and money are now interchangeable, the worth or "seriousness" of music is often determined by the length of the piece. In pop music, for example, the album-oriented era, which commenced with *Sgt. Pepper's Lonely Hearts Club Band,* was considered a dialectic progression from the singles era, and heralded the first serious critical consideration of the form. The pop single had always been dismissed as "bubblegum," with more verbose and long-winded jazz contemporaries receiving critical props.

—

When *Tommy* appeared two years after *Sgt. Pepper's,* it was considered a revelation, the fruition of The Beatles' aborted excursion into opera, the medium long considered the "total work of art." An artist's great statement was always their double LP, as with the so-called *White Album*, Dylan's *Blonde on Blonde,* and the Stones' *Exile on Main Street*. Similarly, the opera that trumped all others in terms of critical respect was Wagner's marathon *Ring* cycle, which lasted five days.

The time = worth equation is present in other forms too. In film, the Antonioni or Kurosawa films which exceed three hours are the most "serious" ones, with David Lean's epic *Lawrence of Arabia* being the studio film par excellence. Warhol poked fun at this conceit with *Empire* and *Sleep*, his unendingly boring static art-house events.

Therefore, the era's obsession with time, whereby each new invention radically contracts the time it once took to perform a menial or supposedly inconvenient duty, such as baking bread or washing clothes, has elected music to its modern, cosmic relevance.

It is a status that can seem bewildering. The holy mantle of music is strange when it seems to have lost its venerable function as Dionysian trance-inducing rite or crucible for community. While ancient cultures used their music for festive mania and for violent incitement in times of war, the modern equivalent can seem abstract and meaningless. Spectators and enthusiasts typically stare courteously while the performers self-consciously execute their work. A concert usually ends without the catharsis or rapture that was once expected to accompany music, with its arcane metaphysical component.

In a world, though, where time is an absolute obsession, where time and money are interchangeable commodities, the listener is so harried, too guilty to meditate or ruminate, that what he or she desires from the music is for it to stave off the mortality which the advertising industry has pronounced is present in every single second. If music can no longer be relied on to induce a whirling-dervish frenzy, it can provide a blanket of cover from the responsibilities of the minute and hour, usually so wrought with fear of death and sexual anxiety. Music has become a sanctuary essentially, a church where one finds respite from time.

Music's function is now in fact merely one of expanding time for the listener against its unceasing contraction at the hands of the industrial sector with all of its "time-saving" inventions and products. Where humanity has lost the ability to reflect and meditate due to the loss of time (in the form of modern convenience), music replenishes (in the form of abstract, "psychedelicized" expanse and mindless repetition which mimics preindustrial work modes).

The time when one was once alone and purposefully contemplative, the time which has been lost to the jet plane, the hair dryer, the clothes washer, and the microwave, is recouped in the form of music, which relinquishes one from modern neuroses: hence its election in the modern era to the place of prominence in the artistic life of the culture.

This freedom-from-time component is used by industry as well—in the department store, for example, where ubiquitous radio lulls one from the anxiety which the products one stares at initially induced. Music as tool for shopping is one of those particularly sinister reflexive ironies.

The industrial age's "time is money" equation, while elevating aural expression, simultaneously destroyed static art as a viable expression in the culture. Due to painting and sculpture's immediate consumptibility, along with their inverted man-hour–to–time viewed relationship (an oil painting or sculpture is a laborious and painstaking process), static art could no longer command its historical dominance in the age of machines.

Static, two-dimensional art hovered in the background while one hurried to pursue one's wretched tasks in the time-obsessed culture and economy, and didn't challenge time as the medium of music did. Music demands the precious commodity and wrestles with it for primacy, earning the respect of the market if not winning outright. Static art, meanwhile, rolls passively into a corner to be consumed at leisure, inciting only contemptuous second-tier status and paternal, high-handed patronage.

Art scholars, jealous of this new aural hierarchy, insist that a time component is still inherent in painting. What of the implied narrative of the static artwork? And what of its place in history and in the artist's development? And the thousands upon thousands of hours of painstaking scholarship based on the famous canvases? Are they not time-consuming and time-intensive? And, furthermore, don't they command more weight than the relatively infantile proliferated music medium?

These hours, while certainly impressive, are moments culled by enthusiasts, and are not primary to the form. They therefore cannot be counted as integral aspects of the art. They are also nothing compared to the millions of hours which music has muscled from oblivion through the medium of amplified radio. An empire colonized out of otherwise inhabited hours.

Duchamp provided a way out for static art by producing his "ready-mades," artworks that were essentially one-liners, and took as long to prepare as they did to conceive. By electing any piece of detritus as "art," he trumped other time merchants and opened a new world of possibility for his peers. This reconciled somewhat the inefficient money/time relationship that had been suddenly fatal to the craftsmen's genres (oil, stonecutting, etc.), but it couldn't deter altogether the painter's inevitable fall from grace.

Modern art is typically still beholden to Duchamp's model. Warhol's industrially inspired art was crafted in his "Factory," where mass-produced silk screens were signed by an army of underpaid and exploited assistants.

Minimalist work (Kelly, Newman, Rauschenberg) and that of a modern-art star such as Christo follow a similar trajectory. The piece is only executed as an afterthought. The idea is everything and it's just as effective to relay the idea verbally.

This sort of art, with its transposition through rumor, needn't be seen at all and is therefore the most valuable, as it circumvents the time it would take to travel and look at entirely. In the twenty-first century, though, it's generally accepted that time-based video art and performance are the future and that still pictures will soon be altogether extinct.

Napoleon III?

SEINFELD SYNDROME

Look to the cookie.

JERRY SEINFELD

TV shows have been stunted purposefully, so as to favorably highlight the commercials they're designed to showcase. While these commercials have developed into a meta art form, surreal and even funny, sitcoms have barely wavered from the anemic model drawn up by *The Honeymooners*: witless plots, stupid jokes, and preposterous canned laughter. Since television's invention, its shows have languished in a state of condescending mediocrity.

In the early 1990s, however, a program of unprecedented charm and intelligence appeared, designed expressly for middlebrow tastes. Called *Seinfeld*, it was immediately discernible as distinct from the rest of the prime-time pack. Set in NYC, it followed the misadventures of four friends who just hung out a lot.

The jokes on it were actually funny, and the writers omitted the requisite life lesson from each episode's conclusion. As opposed to traditional television, which patronizingly instructed the audience as to their correct point of view, *Seinfeld* was like TV's programmers, the ruling class, talking to their own. Leading men "Jerry" and "George" joked with us as one would with a buddy on the golf course.

After decades of televised abuse, viewers responded warmly, even lovingly, to programming that didn't seem to assume their idiocy. After a few rocky seasons, *Seinfeld* assumed its rightful place at the top of the Nielsen heap, and the people rejoiced; finally, good had triumphed over evil.

Following *Seinfeld*'s appearance on network television, urban centers across the country were stunningly "revitalized": property values soared, chain stores invested, and the bourgeoisie scrambled to infest the broken metropoli they had previously shunned. Coincidence? No.

Unbeknownst to *Seinfeld*'s faithful, they were exalting a show with a mission.

Seinfeld was designed expressly to rehabilitate the blighted American city, not only as a place desirable for white people to live (the characters on the show, all white, bear the last names Costanza, Benes, Kramer, Seinfeld, representing a pan-Caucasoid alliance), but as an amoral upper-class playground, where no one need act responsibly or nicely—an anticommunity. On the show, the city is advertised as a place where sex is plentiful and always transmogrifying, owing to the self-replenishing flesh pool that every urban center offers up; Jerry's sex partner, for example, changes with each episode.

Seinfeld's characters, each more loathsome than the last, indulge in a selfishness unimaginable in the suburban milieus of their televised predecessors. Due to the anonymity that the city provides, there is no culpability for their actions. The program's conspiratorial tone of intimate confidentiality stems from its function as proxy mouthpiece for the ruling class through which to speak to its bourgeois counterparts.

The lack of an overt "message" in *Seinfeld* reflects capitalism's code: individualism and self-interest reign supreme. In one episode, when Jerry ruminates over a "black-and-white" cookie, he spoofs a message of racial harmony. "Look to the cookie," he says; ironically, the black-and-white cookie depicts a segregated world, as opposed to fudge-swirl ice cream, for example.

Of course, *Seinfeld's* characters are supposed to be read as the four principle psychological components of one person, with Jerry as the ego, Kramer as the id, George as the unconscious, and Elaine as the rationalizing superego.

The cityscape in this psychological interpretation is their projection of reality, with foreign bodies as irritants, each one enforcing the conceit that humanity, except in the role of sex toy or clown, is contemptible: an enemy agent.

Seinfeld was given the explicit approval of NYC Mayor Rudy Giuliani, who even deigned to appear on the show. In the aftermath of the show, we must consider that Giuliani's notoriously reactionary policies were almost certainly constructed in collusion with the *Seinfeld* program.

Seinfeld, a half-hour situation comedy, which proudly proclaimed itself to "be about nothing," transformed the urban environment completely. The American city had been abandoned by the bourgeoisie as beyond repair: now it was "fun" and "cool" again. This phenomenon, called "Seinfeld Syndrome," is a watershed of our time.

When NBC aired the lowbrow copy show *Friends*, the fate of the city was sealed, as a whole new strata of morons emigrated to its fabled dating pool.

After the *Sein-Friends* had finished celebrating the city's sexual appeal, a program called *The Sopranos* appeared, also designed for the middle class. This show proposed the suburb as teeming with vulgarian mobsters and their tacky molls: no place for Martha Stewart! The preppy migration accelerated.

The cable serial *Sex and the City* helped sway the final holdouts. The triumvirate of shows, *Seinfeld, Friends,* and *Sex ...,* appealed to distinct and specific subsegments of the desired target audience but were united by the singular theme of hawking the city address as a sexy and indispensable accoutrement if one were to be presumed carnal and exciting.

The so-called rehabilitation of American urban centers, which was predicated by the appearance of *Seinfeld,* was in fact a calculated attack on the city, led by the ruling class and fought through its minions in the suburbs, who had laid siege to embattled urban residents for a half century. Like a pillaging army, suburban shock troops laid waste to all they found, precisely recreating the sterile strip malls that characterized their homeland.

As the suburban prefab landscape encroached further toward the city centers, the diversity that had characterized the metropolitan center vanished, unable to resist the virulent weapons of wealth, conformity, and mediocrity. Soon, the city itself was extinct, enveloped completely by its imperialist neighbors.

The colonial arrogance of the suburban bourgeoisie was in fact indistinct from other imperialists through history: the Starbucks they constructed on every corner were echoes of the cricket fields the English had once smeared across Burma.

The city had historically been the enemy of the ruling class. Its serpentine paths and multifarious holes provided the perfect settings for nineteenth-century Bakuninites to raise hell. To protect government from possible insurrection, bucolic cow towns were often chosen to house the precious innards of the various regimes: Versailles, Vichy, Bonn, Washington, Brasilia. But during the years of France's Second Empire (1852–70), Louis Napoleon appointed Baron Haussmann to construct a new, more policeable Paris, which would be the template for the twentieth-century city.

The "Haussmannization" of Paris eradicated two-thirds of the old crowded, asymmetrical, medieval city and replaced it with a place of promenades and parks for the bourgeoisie to stroll and shop. Paving stones, the rioters' weapon of choice in the revolutions of 1789, 1830, and 1848, were covered in modern pavement, streets were widened, and slums were disassembled.

Paris's broad boulevards and defensible circles were vaunted as revolution-proof, designed for easy deployment of artillery and cavalry, and its model was enthusiastically copied, particularly in the New World. But even in the safety of the new city, the working class was still unpredictable, often radicalized, and despicable to look at.

The rise of the Paris Commune (1871) showed that strategic city planning was not a cure-all. With the opportunities presented by WWII's economic upheaval, the ruling class moved to conclusively isolate their ancient proletarian nemesis.

In the late forties, the "Big Three" of Detroit, fat from war contracts, bought and demolished the nation's urban bus and light-rail systems in a lightning campaign to ensure the population's total subservience to their "motor carriage." Lobbying Congress to build the interstate system as a tax-funded "defense" device, they smashed the country's train system. From these insidious origins, the decentralized, suburban American landscape was born.

As the bourgeoisie moved from the newly desolate urban husks, the black proletariat who'd been lured north by wartime industry was economically abandoned, and "urban blight" set in. Riots, actually symptoms of this fiscal terror, were instead blamed as its root cause, as the now-dysfunctional city's wealthy refugees indignantly laid blame on the victims.

"White flight," a term designed by Madison Avenue, was marketed by the auto industry to sell cars after contriving this scenario of interracial warfare. Successful "flight," of course, was contingent on ownership of a reliable car. The so-called middle class became tourists in their own country; they motored about as self-satisfied voyeurs: "I wouldn't wanna run outta gas/break down in this neighborhood" was their mantra as they peep-showed the institutionalized poverty.

The construct of race terror had worked its paranoiac magic in prompting the population to comply with the new unspoken rule: mandatory automobile ownership. Meanwhile, the ruling class's paranoia of the compressed proletariat led them to recreate the city as a concentration camp; instead of Zyklon B, alcohol, heroin, and eventually crack were administered cheaply and efficiently to the inmates. This ensured the modern American city's new role as social scapegoat and tawdry freak show, a place disfigured by poverty and crime: phenomena that were in turn inferred to be synonymous with "blackness." This new race construct of "black" person as marginalized social pariah incapable of rehabilitation was a psychological breakthrough for the ruling elite, useful as invocation for social control.

Generations were weaned on this orthodoxy, indoctrinated via TV serials such as

Sanford and Son, Good Times, What's Happening!!, and their suburban white counterpart programs *The Brady Bunch, Three's Company,* et al. The miscegenation that would rarely occur on these shows always underlined the essential conditions incurred by race; the black children on *Diff'rent Strokes* were poor and from the "inner city," while the white father was a blue-blooded Park Avenue CEO (the eighties version of a plantation owner). All the urban comedies were predicated on the idea that the city was a miserable place, the black man's inherited burden to bear. Later oddities, such as *The Cosby Show* and *Martin,* were merely portents of the approaching gentrifiers.

In 1989, after seventy years of capitalist attrition, the Soviet Union began its collapse: this meant that, in the US and internationally, political discontents were psychologically isolated, radical ideology was extinct, and the threat of the working class no longer raised executives' eyebrows. Meanwhile, with industry exported overseas, there was no need to retain an urban black "underclass" as racial foil to control and manipulate the American proletariat. A year earlier, Larry David and Jerry Seinfeld had begun work on the pilot for *The Seinfeld Chronicles*, the show that would emerge as *Seinfeld* in 1989. Coincidence? Once again, no . . .

The bourgeoisie's abandonment of the city and subsequent return had coincided precisely with the parameters of the Cold War. The suburbs had been presented as a futurist utopia by big oil and GM at the '39 World's Fair, were constructed feverishly under Truman and Eisenhower, and then were suddenly shunned under Clinton, upon the dissolution of the USSR and with the appearance of *Seinfeld*.

Though it was promoted as a sitcom, *Seinfeld* was really a commercial designed to promote the city as the rightful home for the elite. With the threat of class war vanquished, the rulers determined the city to be the most effective device for delivering goods, showcasing products, and inculcating the population with "the Joneses"—the desire to live up to the standard set by the fashion, beauty, and luxury industries.

The city was reimagined as the supermall, its allure augmented by its storied history, born of the diversity which would be abolished. Cheap white labor, in the form of aspiring artists, could be lured via this history, mythologized in books which marketed the city through the very idiosyncratic or marginal character its advertisers had helped to systematically exterminate.

The city's new privileged inhabitants would wear their city's outlaw image as a badge of honor and even venerate it with fervor, fiercely proud of a history they had never experienced, let alone contributed to—like suburbanites living on a Civil War battlefield and boasting about Pickett's Charge.

In a sense, though, they earned bragging rights: the city's premium rents and boutique prices came with this fantasy narrative. Ethnic cleansing would be accomplished via eviction: the mass deportation that had worked so well on the Native Americans.

The indigenous city people, who had survived urban blight, gangs, systemic unemployment, police brutality, the state-sponsored crack epidemic, and PCP, finally met their match when faced with Seinfeld Syndrome.

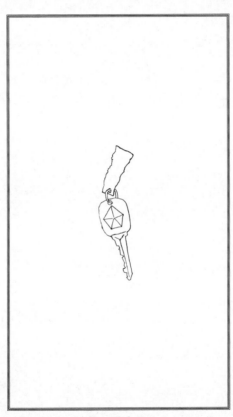

Who Can Afford a Garage?

ROCK 'N' ROLL AS REAL ESTATE

We're a garage band.

THE CLASH

In the early years of the twenty-first century, Alan Greenspan, in his job as steward of the Fed, set radically low interest rates on real estate. This served to fuel manic speculation of housing, and propped up the depressed wartime economy with a building-and-selling boom. The subsequent inflation of property transformed cities across America and displaced millions of poor people.

Greenspan can, therefore, be considered the godfather and midwife to the two paradigmatic indie-music movements of the early twenty-first century: "electro-clash" and its successor, the semiacoustic/psychedelic "folk" revival, both movements based on the new condition—absence of space.

While the two forms are distinct and even aesthetically in opposition to one another, their common aversion to acoustic drums reveals their shared genealogy: they are the fraternal twins of Alan Greenspan.

As popular focus has shifted largely from traditional-style rock "groups" to the new streamlined "folk" or acoustic acts and the one- or two-person computer-programmed "electro" aggregates, we see the old quartet or five-piece splintered, each shard taking a new name in a Balkanized variety of autonomous bodies.

Both the electronic and neo-folk variety are wed not only by a reduction in numbers of the performers (resulting in a larger number of total "groups"), but also principally—and most importantly—by the abandonment of the acoustic drum kit.

Rid of this instrument, with its enormous volume and its attendant need for a PA, guitar amp, and bass amp to match its outsize sound, both formats can be composed, on headphones and at bedside, civilly and in the quietude of high-density living quarters.

This shift has been presented in music journalism as the result of a new awareness of old traditions, but it has really been determined by market forces. The groups now, like the expansive rock groups of the suburban era, are a reaction to, and an expression of, the real estate market and the economy as a whole.

These music trends are a response to a lack of insulated space. Both of these forms advertise the dearth of space, a new kind of living arrangement for most Americans, a poverty which they seek to rehabilitate.

This change was predicated by the abandonment of the suburbs by their traditional bourgeois inhabitants who have now occupied and settled once-abandoned cities. The "folks" and "electros" accommodate the city's new, thoroughly mediocre inhabitants who have their concerns about noise and excitement, having recently transplanted from the controlled environs of the suburbs. The electro-folk acts are typically singular or small, can practice anywhere, and therefore do away with the need for the soundproofed practice space, a hot commodity in any "gentrified" city.

This stylistic transformation, besides exposing electro-clash's debt to Mr. Greenspan, reveals that the rock 'n' roll group has always been an expression of expansion and settlement, linked forever to property and real estate. "Punk rock," for example, began in NYC during a famous economic blight when space was readily available in the form of "lofts." It can be thought of as a form of homesteading or a call to colonization, especially considered alongside the later punk affinity for "squatting" abandoned spaces and transforming obsolete warehouses into clubs.

Like the terms "arena rock" and "bar band," the term "garage band" implies a relationship with space: in this case ownership of a garage and hence a homestead. In fact, the term "garage band" is a euphemism as loaded as "inner-city youth," implying the rockers are members of atomic families with suburban split-level homes and a two-car hutch.

In practice, of course, the garage band

can exist anywhere there is available space or affordable property. The term "affordable" is a relative one and so many of the recent rock groups consist of the best and brightest of their respective country clubs: blue-blooded heirs indulging an interim "wild" phase before they settle into a career buying and selling currencies and countries. These very rich people have inherited the rock band as their plaything to go with the racehorse and the house in the Hamptons. This trend is also manifested in the Hollywood elite, most of whom perform in unfortunate musical aggregates.

—

The rock band declares, "I've got space." Whether it's an invitation for settlement (like early punk) or an advertisement of affluence, the rock 'n' roll band cannot be divorced from the idea of real estate ownership and, therefore, conquest.

Like the orchestras that accompanied European imperialism, the rock 'n' roll band was the soundtrack to America's postwar invasion and occupation of so much of the earth. More than Reagan and his arms race or the Polish pope's revival of medieval reaction and bigotry, The Beatles and their ilk were actually responsible for the collapse of socialism in the East (hence the "Velvet Revolution," supposedly the result of Czech people hearing Lou Reed sing about Warhol's coterie of smack-addicted drag queens).

But just as the rock group has been the most successful exponent of imperialism and rapacious global capitalism overseas, it is also a key figure in real estate ventures inside the country. Was Woodstock and the resultant "back to the land" movement among hippies (dramatized in *Easy Rider*) just an unwitting advance guard for subdivisional developers destroying farmland? Yes.

The new types of microgroups are an advertisement for a new way of living, a new serfdom to be tolerated as the class divide becomes unacceptably large and the specter of homeownership and personal solvency becomes more absurd and unrealistic. They also point to the imperial reversal and the American decline. The only space in America now is cyberinfinitude, to replace the ravaged "New World," hopelessly polluted after a few decades of mindless exploitation.

Rock 'n' roll groups are still being constructed and produced, of course. The garage scene in America is now principally represented in blighted postindustrial centers such as Detroit, which resembles pre-"gentry" New York in a way.

The groups there are nostalgic vestiges of a pre-Greenspan era and the brazen hopes which typified that time.

Ekberg: La Dolce Vita

11

A WARNING
TO SWEDISH GIRLS

London is teeming with lovely Swedish girls, each one manning a post at some bogus internship while riding on their own nation's largesse.

The jobs, which consist of sitting around in some minimally furnished office at a gallery or agency, require only that they act very Continental and look trendy. By day they capitalize on their phlegmatic Nordic drawl. By night they prowl the putrid clubs of the city and mechanically gyrate with their anemic English counterparts. The Swedish government foots the bill for the girls' adventures abroad.

Swedish girls are the most sought-after of all girls, not because of their supposed beauty and blondness but because of the maternal nature of their nation's welfare state. This has an enormous psychic impact on infantilized modern man's desire for security, which, due to barren self-awareness, is displaced as imagined carnal longing.

Their country's neutrality and its wealth also make them very hot. And their nonchalance about sex, born of Lutheran frigidity combined with an early immersion in clinical pornography, makes them seem nonthreatening.

The Swedish girls in London's free labor pool create a snare for other Europeans looking for Swedish girls. A domino effect has resulted in a city lousy with the most licentious scam artists Europe can vomit forth, making it a vibrant capitalist locus. The Swedish girls have made London the indisputable center of Europe, with former contenders Rome, Berlin, and Paris left far behind.

The aforementioned counterfeit jobs aren't the reason for London's allure, of course. Each Swedish girl is actually there in hopes of snaring an English boy: a Damon Albarn or Jarvis Cocker of her very own. The Swedish girls' self-perceived northern isolation has given them an inferiority complex that makes them feel positively provincial. Therefore they are obsessed with being chic. Since all of the continent is transfixed by the newest machination of the English fashion/pop factory, the English boyfriend, like any other chic accoutrement, is a must-have.

The manhood of England, immersed in pools of Swedish flesh, must be beholden to their cunning music press which has facilitated the myth of their interminable swinging modernity. They need only get a bowl hairdo or some fey contemporary equivalent and they're awash in nubile Nords, thanks to a savvy and deceitful media organ.

The Beatles are ultimately responsible, for without them and their psychedelic phenomenon, the country would be revealed as a chilly version of Portugal—a conservative backwater left only with distant memories of imperial glory.

Indeed, before the Fab Four, England was drab and bowler-hatted; their parliament wore wigs, the food was bad, and the morality was stultifying. No Swedish girl would have set foot on its soil. In the innocent days preceding "Beatlemania," Anita Ekberg and Ingrid Bergman were in Italy, almost certainly making love to their respective directors.

This, because Fellini's Rome had been the great city of Europe, with its convertibles, scooters, scarves, and cigarette holders. Paris was a close second with art and Sartre and existentialist superstars.

The English were only an aberrant, half-Teutonic curiosity without any major contribution to painting, cinema, ballet, opera, or symphony. And they were conservative: the art movements that transformed aesthetics through modernism, surrealism, Bauhaus, cubism, et al., didn't include any notable Englishmen. When revolution swept the continent in 1830, 1848, 1870, and 1918, England was placid. Only the futurists approved. In Marinetti's 1910 "Futurist Speech to the English," he upbraided his audience for closeting their homosexuality but lauded their capacity for killing on the high seas.

With The Beatles, the Englishman was, for the first time ever, desirable. He displaced the "Latin lover" who had been the mainstay of Western feminine romantic fantasy since the high Middle Ages when the French and Italians had compiled the *Roman de la Rose* and *The Art of Courtly Love* and proposed the modern concept of love. The Beatles also sparked interest in English fashion and film, and very soon Richard Lester was a bigger name than Rossellini, Buñuel, or Truffaut.

The British music trade papers capitalized on this windfall with a cunningly crafted critical regime, transforming a theretofore teenybop world of pop into a mop-top court of Versailles. Ever since, they've held the continent transfixed with the latest wind change, folly, or foible. The soap operas they created (Beatles vs. Stones, Clash vs. Jam, Judas Priest vs. Queen, etc.) endure to this day.

The Englishman's newfound attractiveness was simultaneously buoyed by their film industry, which fomented their snobbish ideal internationally. Though the stereotypical effete-mannered, ruling-class toffee nose exists now only in the Merchant Ivory films which are sold to Americans, the effect of this proliferated archetype has been enormous in persuading the globe of the Britisher's inherent dashing and "cricket" moral compass.

Due to this nefarious propaganda, the Englishman has enjoyed a position of sexual dominance for forty years now. This sexual dominance has resulted in the ultimate reward by the standards of Western sexual commerce today: Swedish girls. The Englishman reaps the dual prize of erotic liberalism and maternal Euro-communism. However, the Swedish girls would do well to remember that their prized, pouty Englishman may seem to swing and represent all things chic, but in reality, he is the gouty father of the ugly American.

Indeed, this modern culture of awful food, industrial blight, and soft-core imperialism which the Europeans love to decry traces its ancestry directly to Old Blighty. The Americans merely took the baton from their lime-gnawing spiritual masters. It could even be argued that the oft-mentioned "American hegemony" is an Ameri-English one: US dominance on the world stage began at Great Britain's behest with their imperial contraction at the end of World War I. US policies are really US-UK ones, drawing mutual orders from transatlantic corporations. Their perpetual alliance in wars like the ones in Iraq and the Falklands are carried over into diplomacy, with both nations working to undermine the EU, the UN, and the euro currency.

England, because of the enduring myth of charm and chivalry borne of its artistic export, is excused from a history of genocidal crimes, despite offenses that rival Nixon, Himmler, and Tamerlane. Its troops marched every indigenous inhabitant of Tasmania into the ocean, for example. The reason for Europe's pathetic general complaisance with Hitler during WWII? A nearly unanimous hatred of England. Quisling was, for example, first and foremost an Anglophobe.

This antagonism was a result of English dominance of the world via trade and sea power. "Control the sea and you control the world" was the Englishman's boast at the time, a conceit at the heart of modern US strategy. Belgium was an English invention, created to castrate French naval power after Napoleon. Belgium became (like Poland later) an English "protectorate," giving Britain the right to enter into Continental politics at will. Israel is the modern analogy, a state that was initially sponsored by England in order to maintain access to the highly strategic Holy Land. All the contrived states in the Middle East are likewise English Frankensteins, gerrymandered by Churchill to ensure their future economic and/or military helplessness (e.g., Kuwait).

How did the English pull off these fiendish stunts? With the race of violent chauvinists who roam there still.

The English pub on a Monday afternoon is scarier than a Detroit drug war or a Mississippi cross burning, and its tribal rituals more bizarre. The "Chelsea smile," inflicted by Chelsea F.C. fans on their randomly chosen foes, consists of knifing the sides of the victim's mouth into a grotesque, oversized "grin." The Britons throw darts and bricks at their athletes during football matches, sometimes hitting them in the eyes, causing public prostration and misery. Meanwhile, gangs of feral youth conduct their "war on the terraces" with office knives and other awful, ordinary implements. And then there are the English "skinheads" who, for entertainment, "put in the boot." The English sports enthusiast is feared and reviled the world over for his primitive, unreconstructed behavior.

Their nightclubs are little better. When the "lad" spies the "bird" he desires to "shag," he need only bark five words: "Grab your coat; you're pulled." She obediently complies. Is this the world you're prepared for, Swedish girls? I hear your protest now: about the Englishman's innate bravery and the chivalry of the Round Table with its noble hobbits, and Jarvis heroically kicking "Jacko" at the awards ceremony. Well, perhaps that was funny, but Michael Jackson is just a demure child molester with a magnetic nose, hardly the Black Knight.

Of course, it's true that the aesthetic presented by the great English music groups (Kinks, Beatles, Stones, Clash, Smiths, etc.) was not necessarily chauvinist or hooligan . . . but the key to this paradox was gay management. All the aforementioned groups were simple yobs that had theater-connected, modish homosexuals pulling the strings and informing the work. These managers whispered conceptual tidbits into the ears of their dashing young pupils, who would have otherwise been exposed as crazed brutalists. And a gay rock manager may not make an ideal boyfriend.

Perhaps the answer would be if this character could be convinced to manage the relationship. The guy will look good with the hair and anemia while the manager, on his way to constructing the perfect art-school rock combo, will suppress the Swedish girl's man's ultraviolence by teaching him about Buñuel.

The affair could have the aplomb and pretense of The Who, the "mania" and "love" ideology of The Beatles, the dialectic tension of The Clash, etc.

Unfortunately, a manager is expensive
. . . Swedish girls: you'll have to give up 20
percent of your boyfriend. Well, yes . . . I sup-
pose the Swedish government could foot the
bill . . .

SCION-TOLOGY

I. BLUE GENES

Like a rare breed of show dog, celebrities' bloodlines intersect at a thousand points.

Nepotism, not talent or charm, appears to have raised them to their respective junctures of notoriety and wealth. As their family trees crisscross more and more, the telltale totems of incest appear: idiocy, hemophilia, even madness.

The wagons have been circled for too long. The exclusivity of the gene pool has spelled the ruin of Tinseltown's artfulness. All the dream factory can produce anymore are sad remakes of TV serials and dumb comic strips: *Spider-Man, Charlie's Angels,* and *The Brady Bunch.*

The nation's highest office is similarly tainted

by heredity: two more George Bushes wait in the wings for their turn as president, drooling like bikers at a gangbang. The newest Kennedy is a cave-fish who plays the banjo. Meanwhile, rock 'n' roll is lousy with Jason Bonhams, Sean Lennons, and Hank the Thirds.

How did a nation that prided itself on its democratic populism begin to ape its European forebears' blood obsession? The American myth was once one of autonomous self-construction, against the defining role of the family.

The Revolution had spurned England's royal system, and America crowned itself with the grand sentiment "All men are created equal." The nation was rough-hewn, with no "culture" in the European sense, but its democracy gave it moral authority and bragging rights.

As the country expanded in size and power, its people took pride in its vulgarity, electing mass murderers like Jackson and backwoods trolls like Lincoln to be president. Poor immigrants sometimes made millions, joining the mannered "old money" who had a stranglehold on Europe's economy. Multitudes flowed from elsewhere to taste the opportunity the "New World" promised.

As American-style capitalist democracy became the dominant Western paradigm, the old ruling royals in Europe were increasingly seen as arcane and hokey. European monarchies hid themselves away, embarrassed by their anachronistic status, while still secretly intermarrying by night in shuttered, cobwebbed estates.

The English monarchy, with their billions, still strutted about as a public obscenity, but most others, like the Swedes and Belgians, were coy about their anointed, playing them off as you would an unfortunate flatulence. Only *W* magazine curated their shuffling carcasses.

Everyone, rich and poor, envied the Americans for their freedom from etiquette, and their apparent class mobility.

Then, somehow, everything reversed. Americans began to worship Europeans and their supposed "authenticity." They desired the validity that history seemed to confer. They longed for the centuries of religious wars and class stratification that had made the "Old Country" so idiosyncratic, and had given the Euros their veiled neuroses and dark secrets.

Americans, despite their total mongrelization, tripped over themselves to identify their blood origins. The closer one was, in decadence, to the homeland, the more authentic. Before, the boast among white Americans had been a lineage back to the *Mayflower*, or having been a "Daughter of the American Revolution." Now, one bragged of a childhood in Estonia. St. Patrick's Day and its various counterparts have exploded in popularity. Anyone with a European accent is a minor star.

The ideal of the everyman who could grow up to confound expectation and achieve greatness had been, though largely fantasy, a defining American archetype. Now it is a distant dream. The inheritors of wealth and power are everywhere: in politics, business, art, and, most visibly, in the movies.

From every placard on every boulevard, the progeny of the famous beam down at us, announcing their latest celluloid escapade. The names of the stars are all tied to Byzantine dynasties: Sheen, Cage, Barrymore, Paltrow, Douglas, Baldwin, et al., and Hollywood's new "who's who" are their charmless nurslings. Gone are the days when tousle-haired moppets like Lana Turner could be scouted at the soda fountain. Now the casting director is a Nazi doctor, schooled in the pseudoscience of eugenics. What predicated this change, from wild and woolly to wannabe? Is the heart of this Euro-idolatry white supremacy? Or is the answer more complex?

II. NEW BLOOD

Before the Columbian discovery of the "New World," Europe was a wretched, impoverished place. Power was exclusively inherited through families who were exalted as "royal" by "divine right." The population were mostly "serfs," people tied to the land through compulsory service. The food was tasteless and scarce. By the sixteenth century, imperialism (the Venetian sack of Constantinople, Portuguese colonies in Africa, the Spanish conquest of the Americas) had brought revolutionary changes to the continent. The middle class, suddenly illuminated by looted wealth, slave trading, and concentration camps, rose to new cultural prominence.

This newly empowered social stratum jealously reviled the inherited power of the old royals, and sought to exorcise it. They elected new philosophers who would construct ideologies to bring parity between the old inheritors of wealth and power and the new claimants.

Thus was born the "Age of Reason" and its posited notion that "all men are created equal," which found its physical expression in the American and French Revolutions. Though these actions were heavily flavored with "enlightenment" rhetoric and Masonic brotherhood jive, there was no radical redistribution of wealth or power; slaves were still sold, the rich got richer, and the historically poor stayed poor.

After these revolutions showed themselves to be a mere changing of the guards, political philosophers took note. Across Europe, the theorists who plotted the upheaval of society saw that the bourgeois democracy promulgated by merchants and Freemasons was merely a streamlined version of its monarchical parent, an intraclass squabble. The culmination of the French Revolution was Napoleon, while the seemingly delightful Yankees were building an empire in Latin America and exterminating the natives with their white supremacist "Manifest Destiny."

Revolutionary theory addressed this condition, implicating the bourgeoisie with the monarchical rulers. The revolutionary proletariat was seized with bloodlust, which it acted out in the uprisings of 1830, 1848, and in 1871 with the Paris Commune. This kind of ideological brouhaha culminated in the October Revolution, the slaughter of the Romanovs by the Bolsheviks, and the subsequent nationalization of Russian industry. Fear of communist infection gripped the imperialists. The Western banking powers promptly financed an invasion of Russia by fourteen different nations: the British from the north, the French from the south, the Americans and Japanese from the east, and their various running dogs from the west.

All was to no avail. The Reds won this so-called civil war and the Soviet state was consolidated, but not without gruesome death on all sides.

With this development, America heard its death knell. The conclusion of capitalism was, with a few exceptions, the proliferation of wealth within a certain class: a mirror of the old aristocratic system (the Rockefellers, Mellons, Forbes, Bushes, et al.). The royal system had thrived not only from their monopoly of wealth and weapons, but from the Church-led pronouncements about divine right and people's assignations from God. This brainwashing, more than any other factor, had ensured the aristocrats' longevity. Meanwhile, with all its populist sloganeering, the US had actually been advertising for its own destruction.

The ruling class needed an unimpeachable power to remind its subjects of the cosmic scheme and their lowly spot within it, as the pope had for the royals in an earlier era. But semisecular capitalism needed a nonreligious agent to promulgate it.

III. THE FINAL SOLUTION

The aforementioned Russian Revolution occurred during a period of cinematic fecundity in the US that was dubbed, upon its disintegration, "the golden age of Hollywood."

Hundreds of films were produced each year and people went to the cinema at a rate which is unimaginable nowadays, with the multiplex commute, the poor movie selection, and the high ticket prices, not to mention TV, DVDs, et al.

Movie stars had bewitched audiences globally since the medium's initial appearance, and film was widely recognized as a fantastic disseminator of ideology. Fan frenzy for now-forgotten stars subsidized extravagance, not to mention multitudes of programs, "fanzines," and books that proposed to illuminate the details of the various stars' lives.

While actors had been thought ruffians and rogues in Shakespeare's time for their shifty ability to become other people, they were now the most exalted icons of the culture. This because, in their daily job, they enact the unfulfilled promise of the enlightenment and the American Revolution, the ability to radically change one's situation: to transmute from lead into gold.

Movie stars are the carriage for the masses' desire for transformation; the workers long for the ability to metamorphize as these alchemical entities do.

In a stunning assessment of the psychology at work, the American ruling class would use these ephemeral celebrity wretches to remake the royal system of yore, but in an impotent and parodic sense, thus displacing animosity toward the truly powerful while still programming fealty to genealogy through their symbolic proxies. Since these people, publicly recognized as fantastically rich, routinely shape-shifted to become commoners, foreigners, kings, and pirates, the promise of equality was fulfilled, just as "all men are created equal" had promised. And yet these exceedingly equal people were—and are—adored like none other.

The lineages of movie stars would be used as a totem to infer genealogical birthright and eugenic race theory. The "stars" were bred as a pagan constellation designed to imbue the population with a consciousness of their unworth. The seeming normalcy and even mediocrity of this caste, who are rewarded with unimaginable fame and wealth, is meant to instill this inferiority complex in their spectators: obviously there must be something at work which the viewer can't perceive, something mystical or perhaps even magical.

The paradigm of average ordination is Charlie Sheen, son of Martin Sheen.

A revered actor, Martin enjoyed the affection of critical elites and the so-called public. Charlie, then, merely by genealogical serendipity, enjoyed the film career of the accomplished thespian. He was anointed by his father's mantle and now enjoys a life of wealth and carnality, never nuisanced by intellect or artfulness. His remarkable ordinariness was held up to the public as an alchemical expo: even this contemptible everyman is transmuted by blood into an entitled dauphin flower.

In Charlie Sheen's flaccid hammery, the rest of humanity breathes in its insignificant-serf status. And yet he—in his film roles, which are kitsch representations of "normal people," and in actual life as the vessel of mediocrity—is lower than us, bringing him full circle as our equal.

IV. ABOLISH THE FAMILY

This precedent and others like it led inexorably to the presidential scenario of George W. Bush, with all its obvious parallels. The theater of politics is scarcely distinct from its celluloid cousin, and the two often overlap, with stage-managed wars, Madison Avenue PR blitzes, and sometimes even the same personnel, as with Ronald Reagan and Arnold "the Barbarian" Schwarzenegger.

Charlie Sheen's marriage to a commoner, Denise Richards, confers privileged status on her as she moves into this new dynasty. Their scions will be born into the "star system," as this aristocracy is called, a title inferring that their privileged destiny is astrally ordained. Their inevitable intermarriages with other prominent celebrity families will ensure the continuation of the exciting, sexy bloodline by a third generation, by that time "Old Hollywood."

When neophytes do manage to crash the palace gates, they are outfitted with various surgical corrections, as no mere mortal could compete with the perfection embodied by a Drew Barrymore or Gwyneth Paltrow. These surgeries are always grotesque, a self-mutilating penance for impure blood. After the "star" is cycled through the mill, exploited, abused, and discarded, they are filmed apologizing for their impertinence in masquerading as one of the royals. They just couldn't handle the pressure.

We see now why Hollywood has such affection for princess stories (*The Princess Diaries, Star Wars*) and why Disney spent so much time writing revisionist history regarding Anastasia, even after the Cold War was over. One's genetic history or connection to established star gentry is now central to one's future in the dream factory. Family trees will be hung over the casting couch in a shamanistic ceremony to draw the various anointed unwed toward the hopeful starlet's fertile delta.

The bloodlines must be broken and families forcibly relocated, kept ignorant of the whereabouts of their brethren. The children of the Hollywood and entertainment elite must be kidnapped, raised communally, renamed, and reeducated, instead of being allowed to indoctrinate the next generation as to their destined roles due to divine right.

It is the first and most vital step toward a just distribution of the wealth vis-à-vis the whole of society. When you wrench the children from their vulgar mansions in the night, it will be a pitiable thing. Their tears will seem real but you must ignore them; lies and mimicry are their stock in trade. It is what they were bred for.

Initially, the Bolsheviks had longed to abolish the family, recognizing its intrinsically antisocial character, that its motivation was for its own well-being and security above all others. In their envisioned state, children would be raised by the Soviet, for the sake of equality.

Unfortunately, poverty forced the USSR to abandon its futurist scheme in favor of the old, faulty model of familial child-rearing. Their failure has wrought this abomination of celebrity bloodlines that wreaks its terror on us all.

Their failure translates into our terrible and urgent responsibility.

13

MORDOR DEAREST

The 1990s were characterized in film by a feminized machismo: Hollywood's perversion of feminism into a "girls kick ass" philosophy, whereby women killed and maimed on-screen to demonstrate their equality.

This was a reflection of the neoliberal regime that held power at the time. The twenty-first century's retooled war economy and its official nostalgia for the "greatest generation" announced a return to the army-buddy genre and its exclusively male line-ups; *Band of Brothers, Black Hawk Down, Saving Private Ryan, We Were Soldiers, Hart's War,* etc., all iterated that men must now be men again.

This maleness extends into all mass media; Madonna, the Spice Girls, and other various divas of the old era are history, condemned as castrating bitches (e.g., M. Carey's strategically publicized humiliation).

The guys in a gang on a heroic mission, consecrated by violence, is the story du jour and there aren't any lines for the ladies.

That all this coincides with the new, endless war is unremarkable. American film is an obedient propaganda medium. To confuse it with auteurism is naive at best. Just as *Star Wars* set the stage for the final phase of the Cold War, and *M*A*S*H/Apocalypse Now* rehabilitated foreign intervention for the US Army, Hollywood has recently provided a catalyzing series of films to rally support for the rightist Christian holy war and the regime's fear and hatred of women.

These films are Peter Jackson's *Lord of the Rings* trilogy, based on the books by J.R.R. Tolkien. *The Lord of the Rings* fits perfectly into the misogynistic master plan of the dream factory, being the boyhood saga par excellence. Indeed, J.R.R. Tolkien belonged to a Christian men's club, served in the Great War, and preempted Robert Bly in many ways.

The Lord of the Rings has long served as escapism for the awkward adolescent or the sexually confused preteen boy to a fantasy world without women and mothers.

A particularly homoerotic or sexually ambiguous period of rock 'n' roll is synonymous with the trilogy: Robert Plant sang of "Mordor" and the "Misty Mountains," Marc Bolan's Tyrannosaurus Rex featured a member called "Peregrin Took," and Queen's Freddie Mercury synthesized his Zoroastrian faith with hobbit imagery. While Zeppelin supposedly fornicated with middle-school groupies, T. Rex and Queen both toyed with the anti-woman homoeroticism that serves as the basis of so much adolescent boyhood play.

Aside from the trilogy's obvious eugenic overtones and Christo-Masonic symbolism, its hobbits, dwarves, and goblins—supposedly the benevolent domain of so-called nerds—are a cover for a cunningly constructed supermacho ideology. On careful inspection, one recognizes that The Lord of the Rings is the woman-hater's bible.

—

The Lord of the Rings begins in the Shire, the land of hobbits, which resembles nothing more than an idealization of a carefree children's world. Indeed, in Tolkien's milieu the Shire represents childhood, and the hobbits, or "halflings," are children living in a perpetually preadolescent and polymorphously perverse sexual state. They are unattended by parents and therefore frolic in magical shoeless grace.

One day, the famous wizard Gandalf intrudes on the Shire for the hobbit Bilbo's birthday celebration. Bilbo is more worldly than other Shire denizens, having left the comforts of childhood long ago on an adventure (with the wizard Gandalf, in fact), whereby he came to experience the love and companionship of elves, men, and dwarves, and where he discovered a ring of special seductive power.

Bilbo found this ring in a hole, where it was guarded jealously by its owner and servant, a creature called Gollum, who cooed incessantly about its beauty. The ring, which grants the wearer invisibility, helped Bilbo escape from Gollum's hole, as well as some other sticky situations. On seeing his old partner after many years, Gandalf notes that Bilbo too has been driven mad by the power of the ring, calling it "my precious" just as its previous wretched owner had.

Piqued by jealous anger, Gandalf recognizes that the object is in fact "the ring of power," which has the ability to seduce and destroy all life in "Middle Earth," the confederation of fairy provinces which comprise Tolkien's world. The wearer of the ring, despite whatever good intentions, shall be irrevocably drawn into the service of the evil one Sauron, who resides in the dark Kingdom of Mordor.

Gandalf recounts the saga of the ring, how its master Sauron was nearly defeated at the great "Battle of the Last Alliance" by the combined armies of Middle Earth, but that the weakness of man, who believed he could keep the ring for his own use, had kept it from being destroyed.

Gandalf won't even touch the ring, for he knows its power is too much, that he'll also be seduced. For the ring is none other than the dreaded "vagina," poised to destroy boyhood irrevocably and smash asunder the childish prestidigitations of the Shire-land. "Sauron" is actually woman and "Mordor" is motherhood. The "Gollum" is what occurs when a male is entrapped by a girl's charm; he's reduced to a pathetic, cooing parody of manhood.

The vagina is such that good and noble men who think they can flirt with its power and engage in uncomplicated sexual aerobics are ultimately crushed, enslaved, and locked in servitude to Mordor: that is, motherhood and family. Sauron reveals herself as a "flaming eye" that resembles a dangerous fiery vagina-egg hybrid. When the ring is worn, it renders the wearer invisible, taking them away from the boyhood milieu. Sex leads to such a vanishing act, the individual's destruction, and the end of childhood and friendship.

Gandalf recognizes that the only one with a chance of destroying the vagina and not being seduced is the preadolescent and thoroughly homosexual Frodo, who is never without his simpering manservant, Sam.

They are joined by another hobbit couple and embark for the land of elves. Despite his relative strength in resisting the pleasure of vaginal intercourse, Frodo too feels very "strange" when the "ring" slips, as it sometimes does, onto his finger. It obligingly conforms in size to his hobbit hand and provides a frightening peek into the weird, scary world of teenage sex.

The hobbits are pursued by "ring wraiths" or Nazgûl, nine cloaked riders who all wear magical rings of their own, but who seek the great "ring of power" for their mistress, Sauron.

They are former man-kings who, like the Gollum, were seduced and destroyed by carnality. Now they are ghastly, ghostly, pussy-whipped specters, seething with resentment at the freedom their womanless hobbit competitors enjoy. Their leader is called the Witch-king.

As they pursue their prey, they are stopped

at a river by an elfin beauty who dangles her virgin purity before them. As jaded, sexually knowing degenerates, they are shamed into adjourning.

Meanwhile, Gandalf rides to the wizard Saruman's tower, called Isengard, where he hopes to confer about destroying womankind. Saruman, the leader of Gandalf's order and apparently his old lover, is an extremely powerful ally. Saruman, however, is cantankerous, and bitterly gripes about Gandalf's dalliance with Bilbo.

Gandalf's sexual licentiousness has actually caused Saruman to seek commiseration with Sauron, whose sway he is now fully under. On learning of Saruman's treachery, Gandalf and Saruman engage in a heated phallic battle with their staves, and Gandalf is finally imprisoned on the top of Saruman's tower. The gog-eyed Saruman asks his new lover Sauron for instructions, whereupon she tells him to "make me an army."

This is really an instruction to give her children, and soon Saruman is concocting "orcs"—the couple's babies—out of gooey placenta from a hole he has dug in the ground.

Meanwhile, the elves, who represent a sexless, children's idealization of adolescents, have rescued the hobbits from their mishaps and are bitterly condemning mankind/adults for their "weakness," a.k.a. their libido.

In their art deco castle they house a relic from the Battle of the Last Alliance, the sword "Elendil," broken in pieces and representing the castration and powerlessness fated for Middle Earth if the woman threat is not destroyed. This sword/phallus broke when it hit the ring/vagina, yet it sliced off the finger that wore it. Though the penis of the father is easily lopped off, the mother and her vagina are more formidable.

The "fellowship" that goes to protect Frodo on his dangerous journey to wreck the ring includes the hobbits, an elf-dwarf couple, and an argumentative pair of male knights, Aragorn and Boromir. While the one knight is so chaste as to have taken a eunuch elf wife, the other, Boromir, is constantly tempted and tormented by the power of the ring. He finally succumbs to its temptation, whereupon the orcs—Sauron's babies—destroy him. His momentary weakness leads him to fatherhood and banishment from the latently homosexual Tolkien boy-world.

When the fallen knight apologizes for betraying the gang or "fellowship," the other knight lies on him and kisses him gently; the destruction of babies is the duty of the child, for the newborn signals the impending end of his own childhood. "I will not let the white city fall," Aragorn promises, tantrically. (This promise of erectile endurance is important, for it mixes a pledge of vengeful support with a stern chastisement: with a little more discipline, impregnation could have been averted.)

All who come into contact with the ring are tempted by its charm. Even the elvish princess Galadriel briefly imagines herself sexualized through its appropriation; this fantasy of vagina ownership, though momentary, transforms her from lovely coquette to horrible tyrant mother.

Throughout the story, holes are equated with evil and all manner of evil resides in them. The ring is a hole, the orcs come out of holes, Gollum lives in a hole, and Gandalf is finally killed when "an ancient evil" is summoned up from another hole. The ring can only be destroyed by being cast into another fiery hole, atop Mount Doom; Tolkien is proposing here that Creation try again after its folly in forging womankind.

It is important to note that the ring or vagina of Sauron is actually disembodied from her; she is not whole. It is the union of the two that is the great fear. While the sexless Sauron in Mordor has been kept militarily contained by men and elves, the ring has likewise kicked around for ages, fornicated with by randy scamps like Gollum and Bilbo. The mother and the ring, though certainly despised, are known quantities and under control.

But if the mother is reacquainted with her sexuality (the ring/vagina), then it is apocalypse for Middle Earth and the triumph of evil. The mother threat can be tolerated if and only if it is divorced from sexuality. Bilbo's sexual liaison with the passive, lost ring, or Frodo's temptation to screw it in a fit of bisexual hedonism, were weak and embarrassing, but ultimately okay.

It is feminine power and sexuality combined which are the great, insurmountable Satan, and particularly, it is the transference of the boy's feelings for his brotherhood onto his female lover (the surrender to Sauron upon the taste of the ring), resulting in union/marriage (Mordor), which is the destroyer of childhood (Middle Earth and particularly the Shire). Thus the strongly homosexual subtext of *The Lord of the Rings*.

—

The film industry has always colluded with federal aims. Through its monopolization of the means of production, Hollywood has invariably utilized what Lenin called "the most important of the arts" as a commercial propaganda tool that not only corroborates the imperialist power structure, but also complies with federal aims in maintaining myths and promoting policy. The American film industry's obedience with the government in disseminating propaganda for both world wars was particularly striking, when the entire might of the studio system was brought to bear on educating audiences as to their proper perspective.

During the arms race, films like *Red Dawn* and *Stripes* maintained the official myth of the Soviet threat, while *The Deer Hunter, Platoon*, et al., successfully rehabilitated antiwar sentiment regarding Vietnam. Hollywood's old reactionary history of Red-baiting and blacklisting is much publicized, but even in these apolitical and passive times the role of Hollywood in wiping out dissent and propagating ideology is relentless.

Hollywood's promotion of various industries through product placement barely warrants mention due to its ubiquity, but the extent to which the subtext of modern film attempts to affect the ideological system of the viewer is truly remarkable. *The Lord of the Rings* is the direct result of the Ashcroft/Bush born-again, woman-hating White House, and contains a convenient race-war allegory to boot.

Though this born-again agenda seems at odds with the homosexuality latent in the fellowship, it is the enforced repression of their brother love that makes them fight, expressing itself in their violence toward orcs/babies and the various manifestations of women.

This paradox of repressed homosexual brother love and fratricide is at the root of all military action.

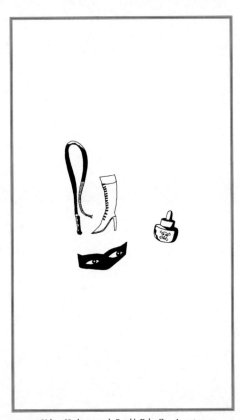

Velvet Underground: Punk's Fake Gay Ancestors

14

CAMP EXPLOITATION

Liberal academia contends that "rock 'n' roll" was heisted from black musical culture, the ultimate example of "blaxploitation." Rock 'n' roll music, it is insisted, is like jazz, an intrinsically black culture, and the white groups who use the idiom are exploiters.

This idea, whereby a music type is considered the intellectual and artistic birthright of one particular segment of society, is now culturally taken as truth, and license to sing or create art of a particular style is permitted only when a special series of criteria are met. Genetic testing is being considered.

At any college establishment, a thousand students bleat for the crucifixion of the "racist" rip-off artists: Led Zeppelin, the Stones, Beastie Boys, etc.

In a startling turn, Jimmy Page was actually

convinced by an angry undergraduate's essay and will now only perform with a harp and a lute: instruments particular to the druids of his genealogy. Other rockers seem poised to follow. It is not known whether these concessions will satisfy the student activists, though.

One collegiate coalition has demanded the immediate cessation of all Caucasians playing rhythmic music. Less radical coeds simply reject the "derivative" stylings of the blues-based rock band for what they believe is the more honestly "white" presentation of "punk" and its various affiliated subgenres.

One of the punk rock movement's central conceits was that it saved rock from this embarrassing wannabe pantomime. It supposedly rescued white youth from hopeless emulation by giving them their own movement, which was as "outside" and provocative as black music, while at the same time it addressed their own, rather different situation.

Punk didn't lift its themes or fashion from bluesmen or soul groups. Punk themes were a "pop" and schizo celebration/condemnation of the alienation incurred by trash culture. Lyrics attempted to shock or provoke listeners with outrageous or grotesque imagery. "Belsen Was a Gas," "Now I Wanna Sniff Some Glue," and "We Got the Neutron Bomb" are all typical punk song titles that were thought of as funny, radical, and rebellious at the time.

These themes had nothing to do with soul or blues music which, regardless of satanic themes, never dealt with pop or contemporary issues in such a camp or absurdist way.

Punk rock was hailed immediately as a movement by bourgeois media scribes due to the coherence of its practitioners' simultaneous vision, which seemed to spring from nowhere. John Belushi dubbed it the "white man's blues." Finally white rockers had forged something original, not cribbed from the African American music scene.

Punk, though, didn't come from nowhere fully formed. Rather, it was lifted directly from another exoticized sector: "gay" or "queer" culture. Rock Svengalis had realized for a while that "black music" was temporarily exhausted as rock 'n' roll source material. Rummaging through their dog-eared tomes of blues standards, they jealously spied the burgeoning gay scene, which had forged a unique and exciting identity. The gay world then was in its heyday of leather clubs, disco dancing, etc., while the "camp" aesthetic prevailed in the arts.

Homosexuality—though creeping into mainstream consciousness—was still very marginalized, so its denizens had the allure and spiritual power of the oppressed, but the connections to make an impact. John Waters and Paul Morrissey ruled the film scene with their provocations, each more vulgar than the last. Warhol, Jasper Johns, Robert Indiana, Ray Johnson, Rauschenberg, and later Mapplethorpe had conquered static and "high" art with the gay "pop art" movement which celebrated trash culture and kitsch. Market-conscious stars Mick Jagger, Lou Reed, David Bowie, and Marc Bolan attempted to pass as gay or at least bisexual.

Like the Jew in Europe or the Irishman in England, the gay artist was an established outsider, reviled and envied as exempt from bourgeois morality.

Meanwhile, rock 'n' roll's perceived relevance relied on its marketing as "outsider" identification, and gay culture was exotic and dangerous, but still familiar. Gay culture was rife with the elements that had originally energized rock 'n' roll: humor, outrage, danger, and dancing. The gay club was absolutely different from a Yes concert.

Though there had been minor gay-ish trends first with the "mods" and then during the "Edwardian" psychedelic era, the first attempt to thoroughly exploit the sodomites was with "glam rock" in the early 1970s. While the glam trend flirted with gender-bending and bisexuality, it was only a management company's dumb fantasy of gay culture: retro-deco, costumey, and contrived, it rapidly lost steam due to its silliness and irrelevance.

Real gay culture at the time was typified by the sexual amorality, black humor, sarcasm, leather jackets, shades, and plastic wear that would define early punk. Meanwhile, Sex Pistols manager Malcolm McLaren's shop (called "SEX") was attempting to make a King's Road trend out of the fetish wear favored by leather boys, hustlers, and perverts at the time.

The Sex Pistols (the premiere punk group) were merely models for the shop; having a group wear the store's products was a stunt or gimmick that was thought to be cheaper than hiring proper dolly birds. They were to dress in this gay gear and play campy old King's Road rock 'n' roll tunes in order to sell these gay clothes to primarily straight, trendy teenagers. Punk was therefore, from the get-go, gaysploitation.

Though punk as we know it came from England, its antecedents were American—punk's celebrated embryos, the New York Dolls and the Ramones. These two groups dressed up as drag queens and gay hustlers, respectively. The Ramones won the authenticity sweepstakes when they confessed their actual experiences as male prostitutes in the song "53rd & 3rd."

Suicide, the template for all postpunk synth duos, were arranged as a bottom and a top. Every duo since has had the same composition, from the Pet Shop Boys to Eric B. and Rakim, whereby the singer is the dandy and the instrumentalist is "trade." While Patti Smith exploited the "butch" lesbian look, Debbie Harry's Blondie focused on the homosexual "camp" style, with odes to B movies and musicals ("A Shark in Jets Clothing," "The Attack of the Giant Ants," et al.).

The English rebuttal to these groups was McLaren's Sex Pistols, who popularized the punk trend. They were named for male genitalia and wore bondage gear. The term "punk," of course, was street or prison slang for a sodomite or homosexual.

Although many of the early practitioners and innovators of punk were gay, punk was initially meant to be a mass pop movement and not the jealously guarded cult phenomenon that it would become. Therefore, the sexual proclivity of these queer pioneers was not typically disclosed for fear of alienating potential customers (as with Darby Crash).

In this way, punk exactly copied its rock 'n' roll twin/nemesis, which appropriated the pose and perceived dangerousness of its black inventors, but whose producers and management prohibited actual blacks from performing the music on a massive scale after its breakthrough.

While punk fashion and graphics (exemplified by Jamie Reid and Malcolm Garrett) stole the black humor and camp style of the gay scene, the music appropriated the vulgarian overstatement fashionable with that crowd as well. Musicianship wasn't important, just attitude. In this way, too, the gay world's creed, whereby theater and presentation were paramount (as opposed to a rock 'n' roll–style obsession with virtuosity and authenticity), became also the byword of "punk."

Of course, punk wasn't an original musical movement (neither was rock 'n' roll) as much as it was a fashion idea and an appropriation of what was then a gay aesthetic and attitude. The haircuts launched a thousand ships; the politics came later. Thus we see that in the same sense that rock 'n' roll was blaxploitation, the punk movement was a mere appropriation of gay culture by a predominantly straight crowd for the purpose of mass marketing a style of rock 'n' roll as rebellion. In short: gaysploitation.

As punk gained popularity, its practitioners, intuitively sensing the limp-wristed origins of their outfits, often turned either sexually moralistic or outrightly conservative. "Queer bashing" would haunt the punk and affiliated scenes. This, ironically, echoes the whole "rough trade" phenomenon rampant in the cruising scene at the time. The punks had unwittingly become "trade," a staple of the gay establishment's collective fantasy life.

Though punk quickly became macho and homophobic, it would eventually balkanize and spawn several "queer punk" movements: a redundancy as strange and ironic as the "black rock group."

As the artsy aspects of bourgeois gay culture were exhausted as source material, "punk" gave way to "hardcore," which was an exploration of gay life in the prison complex, the army barracks, or the seminary school. This movement, lacking the subtlety and wit of the original punk trend, gained massive popularity and eventually, after many years, conquered the airwaves (e.g., Green Day, Blink 182, System of a Down).

While rock still looks toward black culture via hip hop for its inspiration (Linkin Park, 311), hip hop steals from rock and particularly punk rock through image and content. "Gangsta rap" (e.g., NWA) was partly inspired by the violent posturing of LA groups like Black Flag, with their cop-execution (*"make me cum, faggot"*) logo, while Public Enemy was influenced by the MC5 and Devo.

Punk rock's appropriation of gay culture would have profound effects on the queer world, causing it, in a reactionary move, to overwhelmingly reject its patented shock/camp aesthetic and retreat to an exaggerated parody of straight respectability, à la Martha Stewart. Shadowing gay culture as always, punk mirrored this development with the bland, awful, and well-meaning "emo" trend (Dashboard Confessional, Linkin Park, Yellow Card), which also topped the charts.

Does this revelation regarding punk's appropriation of gay culture mean that straight punks should pay recompense to those living founders of their movement: the John Waters and the Paul Morrisseys who pioneered camp garishness, shock, and vulgarity? Or should they stop playing their music altogether? Are they allowed to play punk rock if they just engage in some same-sex sex? Or is an outright conversion necessary?

Angry students at Wesleyan, Hampshire, and Evergreen colleges are holding a conference to determine the answer.

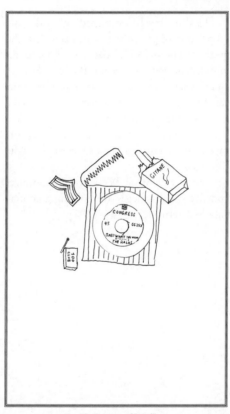

The Detritus of "Mod"

15

THE STILYAGI

Historical revisionists are at work around the clock, assigning false meanings to all events.

Journalism contends that the "eighties" were characterized by unremitting conservatism: a "Reagan era" of young Republicans and preppy fashions.

While these grotesque reactionary phenomena were certainly real, in popular music and fashion the decade was perhaps more progressive or "radical" than anything since. While chart rock 'n' roll music in the 1970s and 1990s was defined by an often macho, blues-based "classic rock," the 1980s were conceived in the shadow of David Bowie and were slavishly devoted to his aesthetic of gender-bending futurist romanticism.

Performers such as Boy George, Prince, Sheila E., Michael Jackson, Wham!, Cyndi

Lauper, Dead or Alive, ABC, Kajagoogoo, Cameo, et al., cross-dressed freely and invited speculation about their sexuality. Implied homosexuality was so rampant and de rigueur that even the hypermasculine metal scene was forced to conform to a transvestite hegemony.

Politics were much more prevalent in chart music from the 1980s, as exhibited by songs such as "99 Luftballons," with the trend culminating in the pithy "We Are the World."

There was also a move away from the blues of rock 'n' roll and toward international sounds, particularly in the UK, as evidenced by records like *More Specials* by The Specials, *Wha'ppen?* by The (English) Beat, and the Europop and calypso-flavored output of Bananarama, Fun Boy Three, and Haircut 100. On the indie charts, the pattern was mirrored by the jazz-tinged records of Tracey Thorn, Stuart Moxham, Rip Rig + Panic, etc.

Paul Weller, who had chart success through three decades, can be examined as an indicator of ideological shifts in the rock 'n' roll genre. His mideighties pop/art group

"The Style Council" was easily the most leftist and conceptual of his three major incarnations.

The aforementioned disavowal of aggressive rock forms was a predictable English reaction to punk saturation, and so when Paul Weller, in the wake of The Jam's split, formed The Style Council, a beatnik café jazz group, it probably didn't raise many eyebrows.

The conceptual nature of the group, however, went beyond its peers in articulating what the other groups merely intimated through style and fashion. Group members Paul Weller and Mick Talbot were joined by a mysterious manifesto writer called "The Cappuccino Kid" who issued wry beat polemics on the Council's record sleeves about the group's "effervescent nature" and their sympathies toward socialism.

The records ran the gamut from light café jazz to disco stompers, revolving lyrically around communist themes of unemployment, postindustrial blight, and international workers' solidarity.

For Weller, the reversal was dramatic. As

the singer/guitarist of The Jam, he had been the commander of the "mod revival" and, as with "garage rock" today or Robert Gordon's 1970s rockabilly resurrection, the movement was characterized by a latent conservatism.

Besides the Union Jacks that adorned the children's jackets, the institutionalized fetishism for particular consumer goods and clothes resulted in a doomed cult of authenticity: the acolytes straining toward a fastidious state of grace that could never be attained due to the fact of their having been born too late. (The original mods ran amok in the early sixties.)

The revival of "mod-ism" was in a sense a defensive posture, protecting English traditions and myths from the barbaric punk hordes.

Weller's new incarnation was not a perverse dive into grimy clobber, though, but another fantasist's role: the paradoxical leftist dandy. The Council's second record, called *Internationalists* in America, was named *Our Favourite Shop* in England: the two names underlining a dualistic affinity for Marxist-Leninist world revolution on the one hand, and commodity fetishism—the capitalist eroticization of the inanimate commodity (which Marx both named and deplored)—on the other. Weller's Gemini "twin" character could never reconcile these disparate urges, but it was "The Cappuccino Kid," a.k.a. Paolo Hewitt, who brought them out to blossom unabashedly.

Hewitt followed in the lines of many aesthetician English Svengalis who encouraged their groups to express their far-out impulses, instead of repressing them in the usual committee-of-compromise band manner.

Like The Clash's Bernie Rhodes, The Who's Pete Meaden, or the Stones' Loog Oldham, Hewitt understood the pop group's role in embodying the unspoken ideology of the moment. Weller's invocation of the scrappy mod hero had been a timely reaction to punk's nihilism, but—as the eighties dawned—the mutually dependent mod/punk dialectic grew tiresome to the trend-hungry English pop hothouse. A transformation was required to avoid extinction. But Weller, addled with superstar status, couldn't simply throw away his street cred with a mercurial, anti-mod volte-face. Therefore, The Style Council were conceived not as a refutation of "mod-ism," but as a revision of its meaning.

Just as the vessels "punk" and "rock 'n' roll" have been endlessly redefined by their various practitioners to mirror their own aspirations, Weller and Hewitt molded their mod-god to a variant more in tune with their own adult lives and the new commercial context. Instead of presenting The Jam's parochial, formalist caricature of the mythic mod lad, they conceived an intellectual aesthete.

Where The Jam had been the working-class disciples of an ideal—the fleshed-out fantasy hybrid of Steve Marriott and Jimmy the mod—The Style Council watched foreign films, read Sartre, drank espresso, and dug Italian furniture.

They also casually propagated world revolution. They explained their raison d'être in the Dalí-inspired film *Jerusalem*, written by "The Kid," Paolo Hewitt himself.

The Style Council made records and enjoyed great success in England and the continent particularly, but by the end of the 1980s they disbanded. The Style Council—fantasist, pop, and effeminate—were self-evidently unwelcome in the authenticity-obsessed 1990s. Weller subsided, but "The Cappuccino Kid" went on to ally himself with yet another version of modernism, "Oasis," who led a movement called "Brit-pop." This movement was an English version of the American "Southern rock" phenomenon, a vaguely nationalist reification of formerly progressive modes. As long hair and acid rock had been co-opted by Alabama, Molly Hatchet, and The Allman Brothers to become redneck symbols, so were bowl haircuts and three-button suits by Oasis for English "lads," that country's anti-intellectual football fans.

Paolo Hewitt became both intellectual progenitor and apologist for this movement, which caught the imagination of the whole of England. Rallying around "the British Invasion" as a period of national pride, Oasis and their comrade groups littered their devices with visual references to that era when England was indisputably at the forefront of pop civilization. Because of the virulent class hatred which pervades English society, none of the intellectual affectations of The Style Council were brought along with this new revised version of mod, but neither was the hopeful punky vigor of The Jam. Oasis wrote "anthems" seemingly designed for jeans commercials: mediocre knockoffs with idiotic lyrics about being famous.

Because Oasis's idea existed in tandem with the mythology of English mod-rock (much as the Stones' mystique relies on the idea of "the blues"), they attempted to resurrect some of their bowl-haircutted forebears. With Hewitt's help once again, Weller's career was dusted off, and he recast himself as a rugged singer-songwriter of indistinction. In conspicuous alliance with Oasis, his now-dull records sold respectably and charted high. The English press respectfully and solemnly call him "Modfather."

Weller's long career, with fantastic success across three past decades, does serve as a barometer regarding fashions and attitudes. As such it undermines assumptions about the presumed conservatism of the 1980s. Of his three major incarnations, Weller's eighties character/group The Style Council was by far the most conceptual, the most politically radical, the most effeminate, and certainly the most interesting.

THE SEDUCTION OF
PAOLO HEWITT

The Oasis Story

CHARACTERS:
Paolo Hewitt
Alan McGee
Bonehead
Corpse I
Corpse II

ACT I. SCENE I.

The Castle of Alan McGee. Scotland. 1993.

BONEHEAD: Master, you have a visitor!
ALAN: No one disturbs me while I'm working! Send him away!
BONEHEAD: But Master, it's Paolo Hewitt;
he says he has an appointment . . .

ALAN: Paolo Hewitt? The Cappuccino Kid? Why didn't you say so? Send him in!

PAOLO: Hello, Alan.

ALAN: Do come in, Paolo, and make yourself comfortable. Would you like a glass of wine? Some brioche? Perhaps a black beauty?

PAOLO: An espresso, please, and maybe a biscuit of some sort.

ALAN: Bonehead! A double espresso and a biscotti for Mr. Hewitt!

BONEHEAD: Yes, Master!

PAOLO: So, Alan, why have you called me here? What's cooking for the Creation label?

ALAN: Actually, it's my greatest "creation" of all! Come, step into my laboratory . . .

ACT I. SCENE 2.

Into the Laboratory. Two Cadavers lie on the tables.

PAOLO: This is the new group you've signed to Creation?

ALAN: Yes, they're fantastic! I call them "Oasis."

PAOLO: But they're just mutilated corpses . . .

ALAN: Yes, we're still in preproduction.

PAOLO: Where did you find the bodies?

ALAN: In Alabama.

PAOLO: They actually look familiar. Wait a minute; isn't that Steve Gaines and Ronnie Van Zant of Lynyrd Skynyrd?

ALAN: Yes, yes, with modifications, of course.

PAOLO: Modifications?

ALAN: Yes, to get the perfect composite for this new project, we took a forearm from Badfinger, a stump from Malcolm Owen, even a few toes from John Lennon, but it's mostly Skynyrd: with mod hairstyles, of course.

PAOLO: But Skynyrd is a Southern rock band; Creation is a quintessentially British label . . . What's the connection?

ALAN: Can't you see, Paolo? Skynyrd took the aesthetics, the drugs, and long hair from the hippies and tied it to conservatism, nationalism, and a working-class sensibility. It was a multiplatinum strategy that'll work here too! Only instead of "Southern rock," we'll call it "Brit-pop."

PAOLO: You're crazy; it'll never work!

ALAN: Crazy? They called me crazy at Warner Bros., too.

PAOLO: But what about their minds, Alan? Their identities?

ALAN: The brains come tonight, after the Man City/West Ham game; Bonehead will seize them from some wayward hooligans.

PAOLO: But then they'll just be common footballers; that's not rock 'n' roll, Alan! Rock 'n' roll is art school and style and ideas. Rock 'n' roll isn't hooligans and lads!

ALAN: It is now, Mr. Cappuccino! I guess you'd better switch to Maxwell House! Hahahahaha!!!

BONEHEAD: Master, the brains are here!

ALAN: Excellent! Place them in the skulls, gently.

BONEHEAD: Yes, Master.

ALAN: Gently, I said!

BONEHEAD: Sorry, Master.

ALAN: Now crank them up toward the light-

ning; electricity will give them breath
again!

ACT I. SCENE 3.

*They crank the bodies up toward the sky; light-
ning and thunder crash.*

ALAN: [*Shrieking*] LIVE, OASIS! LIVE!
MAKE BRITAIN GREAT ONCE MORE!
[*Starts singing "Rule, Britannia!"*]
PAOLO: It's the apocalypse! Lynyrd Sky-
nyrd co-opting the beloved symbols of
modernism!
ALAN: It has to happen, Paolo; without rock
'n' roll, England is just another Portugal!
To regain our global preeminence, we need
Oasis! But we can't do it alone. We need
your help . . . We need your writing!
BONEHEAD: Master, the rain has stopped!
ALAN: Bring them down, Bonehead!

*They bring the bodies down from the roof.
They're speaking nonstop.*

ALAN: They're beautiful!
PAOLO: They do look quite stunning, actually.
ALAN: Listen to them!
[*Cadavers are speaking loudly and idiotically.*]
PAOLO: It's wonderful!
ALAN: I can feel England swinging already!

[*Cue music: Oasis "Roll with It"*]
[*Fade to black.*]

FIN

The End of Brenton Wood–Sparked Disco

17

THE MIX MASTER RACE

Understanding the DJ Phenomenon

I. THE FUNCTION OF ART

Art that attains paradigmatic stature is presented historically in a variety of ways. When posited as representing the inexorable expression of a collective cultural shift, it's the unconscious murmur of the mass. Usually, though, it's presented as the triumph of an idiosyncratic personal vision and/or a rebellious foil to accepted values. The historian/salesman often employs a conspiratorial tone when art movements or phenomena are being sold.

The pitch usually involves a "status quo" and rejection of the visionary by these conservative establishment philistines before the eventual recognition of the particular artist's genius. The invocation of the "status quo" is instructive here, for though countercultural instincts lead us to assume that this implies a condemnation of the ruling class, the fable of the artist is actually a story about the bourgeois' heroic struggle against proletarian provincialism. The myth of the artist is the myth of culture's leaders.

In fact, popular art always reflects the ideology of the ruling class, and is used by them to corroborate their position of dominance in the culture. The forms or mediums that attain popularity are determined by the ruling class through their monopolization of the channels of mass proliferation and their control of history. Art is used to posit idealized forms and aesthetics as totems to explain and celebrate class relations. Supposedly rebellious forms of popular art, such as rock 'n' roll, reinforce and romanticize the consumer/producer ethos of capitalism, while fine art's postmodern vacuity enforces the regime's anti-ideological stance.

Fine art also serves as a moat between the bourgeois and the proletariat; its inherent and purposeful impenetrability serves its patrons like a gated community and simultaneously explains their superiority through implications of depth and difficulty.

This observation, obvious enough, is remarkable only for the degree to which the artist, in every turn of his development, has shape-changed to mirror his bourgeois patron. The artist's role is so central to the rationalization of class difference that the bourgeois, in his patronage of the artist, has methodically fostered each of these changes.

This "twinning" of the artist to his patron has been constant and consistent, from the artist's inception as heroic painter/sculptor during the Renaissance, to his turn as singer/musician, on to his current role as DJ, in which the artist-as-consumer is exalted for his taste. The painter/sculptor mirrored the endeared manufacturer/merchant in the Renaissance, while the industrial era exalted the musician and his factorization of art through mass-produced records.

The sudden elevation of the "disc jockey"

(someone who merely plays or manipulates records) from his traditional role as party/club–attaché/hireling, into the elite ring of artist/magician is therefore remarkable due to the alienated relationship of this artist to his work, which in fact mirrors the new postindustrial economy of the first world.

Before the ascension of the DJ, the artist was always a producer. Now, as DJ, the artist is a mere amalgam of whatever his purchasing power begets.

This development marks the most significant shift in the construction of art since "art's" inception. The DJ-as-artist echoes the new role of the bourgeois as stockbroker/trader/designator-of-worth and handler-of-commodities. With the exportation of industry to the third world and the new role of imperialist as loan shark/investor (World Bank/IMF), the grooming of the DJ as high-priest/star-artist is a necessary part of ensuring the culture's aggrandizement of the broker and the subsequent denigration of the actual manufacturer.

II. BEFORE ART

During the Middle Ages, artists were workers, employed by the Church to propagate its vision of the world, of which it was the center. The Church controlled politics and determined the content of art, writing, and philosophy. The artist was as likely to sign his work as a cobbler or bricklayer, as he had no identity above or beyond other craftsmen. Adjunct to the Church was the precapitalist feudal system, with its kings and inherited nobility, whereby (in a relationship born of coercion) small producers ("serfs"), using a labor force derived from the family, would pay rent using a portion of the crops they produced on a lord's land.

In this subsistence economy, with very little actual money or surplus capital, the artfulness of the people was expressed practically through everyday things, such as textiles, folk songs, or metallurgy. The Church and the state reinforced one another; the Church constructed a morality rationalizing state oppression, while the state repaid this with political violence (the Crusades, for example) and boon work.

III. INVENTION OF THE ARTIST

The transformation known as the Renaissance changed all this. The Renaissance, emblematized by its mascot "artists," was really the takeover of royal power by a new bourgeoisie class. Beginning in Italy, it spread later through the Netherlands to the continent, and was initiated by the sack of Constantinople in the Fourth Crusade.

Financed by the Doge of Venice, the Fourth Crusade looted Constantinople, destroyed Byzantine primacy in trade, pillaged Eastern Orthodox wealth, and vastly inflated the power of European merchants (particularly maritime), who had been backwater actors for centuries.

The learning of the Byzantine world, jealously reviled for centuries by theretofore crude

Europeans, was finally surveyed benignly by the engorged usurpers.

With its direct lineage to the Roman Empire, the Orthodox empire had never lost touch with the ideas of the ancient Greeks, ideas that were now appropriated by Italian mercantile marauders.

This coup inspired financial adventures on the part of other states. Most significant was the discovery and exploitation of the "New World" by the Iberians in the fifteenth century, which resulted in the seizure of Aztec and Inca wealth and the subsequent establishment of huge slave states. Almost simultaneously, the first European mines and trading posts were established in sub-Saharan Africa.

Along with Spanish galleons full of loot, the establishment of a "triangle trade" between Africa, Europe, and the Americas brought new commercial possibilities to the continent. An unprecedented infusion of capital prompted revolutionary changes in the European social structure. A new moneyed class arose that amassed great fortunes from slave trading and mercantilism, ventures newly profitable as the horizons expanded.

This new so-called middle class jealously reviled the inherited power of the old royals and sought to exorcise it. They elected philosophers who would construct ideologies to bring parity between the old inheritors of wealth and power and the new claimants (themselves).

Thus came the "Age of Reason" and its posited notion that "all men are created equal," ideals propagated by secret societies such as the Freemasons and culminating eventually in the bourgeoisie's seizure of power (Magna Carta, American Revolution, Napoleon, etc.).

Precipitating this political upheaval was the cunning invention that allowed it: the modern "artist," the genius individual who posits his own vision of the world through his art. This artist was designed as a reflection of the newly emerging ruling class: male (traditionally feminine arts such as textiles were classified as "crafts") and self-constructed (not inherited, like the nobles).

Most significantly, however, he was a producer. The artist was elected to be the star of the new culture because he, like his bourgeois benefactors, was a manufacturer and seller of things: a small-scale but highly romanticized version of the "capitalist" merchant/speculator or captain of industry. The alienated relationship between labor, value, and money which informed the merchant's newfound fortunes was also inherently manifest in the artist's work (due to art's abstract social role and also its impracticality), and even exaggerated if he attained great success, leading to the fantastic inflation of so much art.

The artist would eclipse the heroes of former years, the soldiers, kings, clerics, scholars, and philosophers who had dominated the life and mythology of the ancient and middle worlds. Because there was no production component to their work, the new ruling class relegated these former mavericks to mere retainer status, a position they still languish in today.

Under the new system, commerce and industry usurped the role the Church had inhabited in the Middle Ages (employer of the state for use as protector and errand boy). The Reformation and the subsequent religious wars were manifestations of this struggle between a Church-led hegemony (Catholicism) and the new bourgeois mercantile forces (Protestantism).

This civil war raged for two hundred years across Europe, and the demarcation line between the ideologies persists in some sense till today. The precipitation of this upheaval was the Renaissance, before which there was no "art" as we know it. "Art" and the idea of the "artist" were born from the money which Europe begat from imperialism and piracy. Before this, what we call art had an everyday social function. After this, the artist was a secular holy man, who created relics imbued with mysticism and purported to hold a relevance and worth beyond what was immediately apparent.

This power could be granted and rescinded at will by the ruling class. They had contrived the artist as a special caste, whose labor existed outside work. His new function had the cause of segregating him from regular society, as his work served no function other than the exaltation of the bourgeois-led hegemony. Typically poorer than the worker, yet lauded by the ruling class as above the worker, his labor was no longer "work" but "art," which meant that its value was nebulous, determined by the artist's creator—the patron and benefactor.

This idea of art as separate from work and more akin to world-making serves as another reflection of the bourgeoisie's self-image as demigods.

It would be the merchants (the Virginia Company, the Dutch East-India Company, etc.), not the state, who would colonize the earth from the sixteenth century onward.

IV. THE ROLE OF THE ARTIST

On seizing power from the Church, the bourgeoisie replaced the priest with their own shaman: the artist. And just as the monk or priest had enjoyed a special relationship and empathy with God, this new witch doctor was sensitive to the workings of the omniverse. He was "touched," a sort of sexy village idiot, albeit one who led the way through morality's twists and turns. The artist typically painted portraits of his benefactors, battle scenes glorifying the conquest of the empire, or other fluff, which propagated the ideology of the new religion of money and power.

The artist, as industry's servant, would be ordered to innovate. After all, the creation of need is the cornerstone of the market economy. The first "discovery" by the new artist class would be "perspective," whereby the drawer/painter drew lines to a horizon and sized objects in the painting depending on their distance from the foreground. This immediately colored the Renaissance artist as distinct from his craftish medieval forebears, who had drawn all things flat and equally sized, or sometimes sized in accordance to their relative importance in the pictured narrative.

This "innovation" informed the subsequent behavior of the capitalist artist-star: embracing change as valuable for its own sake.

Perspective had been rejected before in paintings, reliefs, tapestries, and mosaics because of its ineffectualness in conveying ideas, not due to a lack of talent or sophistication on the part of medieval and ancient renderers. The highly stylized flat convention of earlier works was more graphic and immediate, much like the comics and posterization popular in advertising and art today.

Renaissance artists contrived this great "discovery" as a simple identity device, a way to mark the territory of the new ruling class and themselves as a new and special caste. This obsession with originality and identity, unusual at the time, was a totem of the age to come, whereby the new persona of the "individual" was given great importance (da Vinci, Michelangelo, et al., signed their work). The moral code demanded by the new mercantile-Protestant ideology to ensure efficiency would relegate tradition and community to a peripheral place, as the hero-merchant clambered forward to grab for himself what would be his. Thus the new, audacious signature.

Though the artist sometimes gained renown in his own time, he was beholden to powerful patrons, had a very short leash, and often struggled through life to die in penury.

V. IMPERIALISM

As the empires of Europe expanded to Asia and Africa, the ruling class became richer still, and the artist's endeavors were made to reflect it.

Painters like Titian employed teams of laborers to execute cosmic scenes. Classical music pleased the powerful, as they saw their role nobly reflected in the composer's stewardship of his subjects, particularly when he waved his stick at them like a god-manager. So-called classical music hearkened to a Greek tradition of formal purity, and was intended to infer white supremacy and promulgate colonialism as not only the entitled right of Europeans, but also their responsibility.

Opera was the enormously stylized and scientifically executed enactment of European ritual and myth, with racial ideology a huge aspect of its intent. Opera was the conduit for its benefactors to expound their ideas and thought systems, such as with Mozart's *The Magic Flute,* an undisguised Masonic tract.

The artistic fusion that opera enacted represented the rise of nation-states and their imperial global systems. The pretensions of classical music and opera are carried on through rock 'n' roll music today, a medium which, among other things, is an exact synthesis of African ritual music and the ideological and highly systemized concepts of the German classical composers.

Classical music's appearance actually coincides with the beginning of the European imperial adventure, while the beginning of the neocolonial period (the end of World War I or the "Jazz Age") signals the end of this music's position of primacy as cultural narrative.

The abandonment of full-scale imperialism was inspired, like so much, by the economic model of the US. With the capitalist-industrialist North's triumph in the Civil War, imperial nations noted a model wherein a triumphant power (the North) needn't occupy the defeated state (the South) to command its economy so long as it controlled it via corporate ownership and political influence, wedded with the believable threat of violence. Likewise, it was noted that wage labor was a more risk-free economic enterprise than slavery or serfdom.

Though the implementation of this US model took another century for many European nations (such as France with Algeria and Britain with India) due to egotism, nostalgia, and conservatism, it was accepted as inevitable long before.

Because industrialization signaled the end of the old style of imperial occupation, it also signaled the end of those art forms that glorified and explained that pursuit.

VI. INDUSTRIALIZATION'S EFFECT ON THE DEVELOPMENT OF ART FORMS

The artist's work was always ordered to reflect the technologies that the industrial producers were hawking. New inventions were utilized regardless of their impact on the quality of the art. With the harnessing of electricity, for example, acoustic music was essentially abandoned, another factor leading to the death of classical music.

These kinds of changes are hailed by historians as reflections of changes in the social order, manifestations of the artist's prescient gift. In fact, these developments are always ordered by industry, and artists who don't comply are shut out, denigrated as irrelevant, or ignored. The artist must act as envoy for industrial innovation since he or she is its greatest exponent, a supersalesman with a pretension of autonomy and the aura of a prophet.

As art's very constitution was ordered to reflect its benefactors' exploits, industrialization directly informed what sort of work would be valued as art. With the invention of the press, print and painting engaged in a struggle for primacy. While painting reflected the capitalist conceit of the preciousness inherent in rare objects (i.e., the gold standard), printing trumpeted the new era of proliferative mass mediums and industry's more direct role in sponsoring them (*nouveau* posters, etc.).

Industrialization also spawned a revolutionary consciousness among artists as well as workers. To an extent, this progressiveness still mirrored the Masonic-bourgeois sensibilities of the patron, as provincialism and reaction through most of Europe (Russia, dual monarchy) were the enemy of liberal commercial aims. Eventually, however, this fostered radicalization would get out of hand, as it did in Russia in 1917, and result in a reordering of the artistic pecking order by the boss class.

With the class consciousness spurred by industrialization, artists, like workers, banded together against his natural opponent, the exploiter/employer. Painters began forming unions (Dada, surrealists), which decreed the ideological parameters of any affiliated work in an attempt to discourage compromise and to affect change in the social order. For the first time the artist recognized the nature of his pursuit, a blend of magical invocation and political warfare.

In this highly politicized era, art was no longer a mere conduit for the ruling class through which to reflect its worldview. It became a struggle for the ideological mind of the industrialized world, as well as for what that world would look like in the future.

Just as the October Revolution in Russia threatened capitalism itself, art had finally broken free from the suffocating patronage that had defined its entire life and drew up in all its forms: from revolutionary suprematists to futurists, fauvists, Dadaists, surrealists, constructivists, Merzists, expressionists, cubo-futurists, etc.

As the artist was thus transformed by industrialization and revolution, so were the bourgeois, who gradually abandoned the painting artist as their ideological foil. Infested by Reds, he no longer seemed a supplicant enough proxy.

In this apparent twilight of the painter as priest, the few who were permitted to survive would mirror industrial capitalism's obsession with renewal.

Inherent in capitalism's structure was the construction of new fashions, styles, and fads, all meant to accelerate consumption and maximize profits. Painters were compelled to mirror this shape-changing, or find themselves used up and thrown away. Successful twentieth-century artists therefore created multiple personas for themselves through frequent stylistic and even philosophic changes, as with Pablo Picasso and Marcel Duchamp.

An artist rebuffed by one of the various radical schools, such as Dali by the surrealists, was sure to be embraced by the capitalist establishment, as was the case much later with celebrated "dissidents" in the Cold War (e.g., Arenas, Havel, Baryshnikov).

VII. THE ASCENDANCY OF RECORDED MUSIC

The invention of mass recording devices and their proliferation broke the back of this struggle, rendering all aesthetic-ideological discussions academic. With the utilization of the phonograph as music box, the musician was suddenly transformed from suspect/degenerate/entertainer to hero/artist.

Overnight, the recording artist eclipsed the visual artist, who was reduced to a beret-wearing caricature. The musician rose to prominence because the new industrialization of the trade (record manufacturing), along with the mechanized synchronization of the music group, mirrored the factorization from which its benefactors drew their pay. Industrialization had swept the West, and the overlords saw in music groups and record makers a romantic specter of themselves, as well as a powerful exponent of industrialism and globalism (then called "laissez-faire capitalism").

Product, whether via advertisements or as aural art, could be transmitted via radio to even the most remote hole. The relative cheapness of the record album made it accessible to a huge variety of people. In the live context, the musician as merchant was capitalism's great evangelist, holding sway over hypnotized consumers with the fascist's best friend: amplified sound. In the concert hall, the performer/spectator relationship was a direct corollary to the producer/consumer relationship of capitalism, hawked in a hermetically sealed showroom with no room for dissent.

Forms of music changed as groups shifted, according to the technology they were made to utilize. These technological changes also reflected the quest in industrial capitalism to streamline production, thereby maximizing profits and minimizing costs. Electricity would serve to hasten this process, though it can be traced in the downsizing of orchestras into "bands," followed by the ascension of bop over swing.

Rock 'n' roll, the synthesis of white hillbilly music and black blues, was greeted with derision at first by a jazz-loving public, but was muscled into paradigmatic status by the music industry, which recognized its promise. The electrification of the instruments meant that a trio could sound, in the words of Buddy Holly, "like an orchestra." Thus fewer session men to pay.

Simultaneously, the relative simplicity of the form smashed the jazz player's guildish exclusivity.

In jazz, the listener was snobbishly aware of a particular player's style and abilities, giving technically remarkable artists a certain degree of negotiating power. The early rock 'n' roll players were anonymous sidemen, hired and fired in droves.

VIII. ROCK 'N' ROLL = NOTHING/EVERYTHING

Rock 'n' roll's main appeal to industry mavens, however, was its supposed youthfulness. Despite the advanced age of many of its original progenitors, rock 'n' roll was marketed as teenybop youth music, and its stars as rebel-idols in the vein of Marlon Brando. This youth angle mirrored industrial capitalism's conspiracy to promote products of planned obsolescence. Every teen star had a built-in time limit, and record company execs were the only ones with stable jobs. This was the best property scam since the Church invented the celibate priest.

Rock 'n' roll groups exposed various electronic gizmos as they appeared. Each Ventures record was an advertisement for a new "fuzz" or "wah" attachment to the electric guitar, which would then become a requisite item for the enthusiast. Rock 'n' roll was a truly liberal art form, embracing any and all stimuli which it happened upon, incorporating them to its form.

Musical genres had previously been defined by a particular instrument or rhythm that made them distinct: rock 'n' roll ignored such parameters, successfully colonizing gospel (secularized as "soul"), folk and country music (folk-rock), jazz (prog), theater, opera etc. Eventually, it was only discernible as a form by the race of its practitioners (typically white).

Rock 'n' roll shows heisted theater's elaborate productions, poetry's words, the printer's designs, and the avant pretensions of the painter. It was Wagner's "Gesamtkunstwerk," which swallowed all art and made it one. Thus, rock 'n' roll professed no creed except secularism and desire: the twin pillars of capitalism.

IX. THE BLUES

Rock 'n' roll was mainly derived from the Southern African American rebel music known as "blues," which posited itself against that culture's gospel paradigm. Blues music rebuked the institutionalized God-fearing pious lifestyle and opted for stories that were macabre and swaggering. The lyrics concerned themselves with infidelity, alcohol, voodoo/magick, and dying without redemption. In essence, the blues was the progenitor to LaVey's Church of Satan, with its earthly emphasis on acquisition and individualism.

Industrial capitalism's boss class chose to rehabilitate this music in an electric version through white musicians. It would be ideal to serve as their soundtrack, as it mirrored their ideology more resonantly than the swinging sociability of jazz.

Rock 'n' roll themes and expressions still slavishly ape the blues model, with most deviations falling into disfavor with the official arbiters of taste. When folk music was revived in the late fifties, its new form shed much of the political and story aspects which had originally characterized it and was encouraged to promote a mythology of "ramblin'," or nihilism.

X. THE GROUP AS CORPORATION

In the beginning of rock 'n' roll, the artist was either a star/singer or a featured instrumentalist like Duane Eddy. Soon, these characters were replaced by "groups" who more resonantly mirrored the boss class. The group was a construct that sounded large, democratic, and inclusive, but was by nature actually fixed and exclusive.

More importantly, as with a board of directors in the industrial superstructure, the group had no culpability; its multifaceted and liquid person could slither from scandal and irresponsibility in an eternal buck-passing session.

It took a collective name, which would serve as a brand or corporate flag and which could sometimes be used to designate a succession of personages.

Even individuals were encouraged to adopt "trademark"-style names (as in "Little Richard," "The Big Bopper," and Phil "Spector"). In this way, the performer once again mirrored the boss class, whose real identities by now were obscured by sinister corporate titles.

In the sixties, which was the height of group culture, groups undercut the radical left by using liberal capitalism's ethos of individuality and apolitical apathy. Democratic capitalism's sloganeering about market liberalism ("freedom") was spiced up with the promise of Hefnerian sex ("love and peace") and successfully used to negate the burgeoning political movements in the country at the time.

XI. THE REHABILITATION OF PAINTING

By electing popular music to replace static painting as the culture's most heroic art form,

the ruling class effectively smashed the negotiating power of the unionized painting cells.
But painting and static art in general were
still useful in the sense that their value never
purported to represent any popular mandate,
making them ideal for rationalizing class difference. They were also still considered relevant to the revolutionary intelligentsia, who,
because of their upper-strata origins, had inherited the bourgeois awe of the artist.

The first capitalist rehabilitation of the
painter occurred with Jackson Pollock and
the abstract expressionists, who were used
to propose individualist and heroic ideology
to a postwar Europe flirting with socialism.
Subsidized secretly by the state via the CIA,
abstract expressionism was explicitly apolitical, concerned only with aesthetic and spiritual issues. Its existence was meant to refute
socialist charges that capitalism couldn't
foster an avant-garde, and also, by attaining
paradigmatic status, to destroy the power and
credibility of agitprop, surrealism, and social
realism (communist avant-art).

Soon after abstract expressionism appeared, an explicitly procapitalist art was promoted under the name "pop art."

Pop art celebrated industrialism, products, and celebrity, providing the materialist rebuttal to the supposed spirituality of the abstractionists. This "pincers movement" by these two nominally opposed but secretly cognate groups encircled the art world in a mirror of the two parties of the American political system, who say the same thing but in different ways. The promulgation of these American fraternal twins was the final defeat of the leftist European avant-garde, already reeling from disappointment with Soviet communism and economically hobbled by the mass destruction caused by the war. The Marshall Plan funded an American cultural invasion of Europe, successfully crushing aesthetic resistance. Through the proliferation of culture and products, the imperialism of the US would be rehabilitated as sympathetic (e.g., *Big Wednesday* and *Uncommon Valor*).

Art transferred its center from suddenly

provincial Paris to the commercial hub of New York City. Ever since, it has been the complacent lapdog of corporate masters.

XII. PUNK AS PINKERTON

Just as visual artists during industrialization had clamored for freedom from stultifying patronage, musicians in the late 1960s and early 1970s vied for better treatment. Their marginalization as "artists" meant that, without the rare wind at their back, they were mere bums without health care or security. With rock having assumed paradigmatic status, the players resisted their whimsical mistreatment at the hands of record honchos.

The arrival of "album-oriented rock" and the nurtured careers of post-Beatles acts had translated into actual leverage against record company dictums. Rock and disco stars demanded fair portions of the profits they were entitled to. As the music had liberally extended to all age markets, the age of the artists had grown correspondingly. Therefore, issues of family security dogged the rock 'n' roll workforce.

These same concerns had sounded the death knell for jazz twenty years before as jazzmen, famed for their skill, had asked compensation for the profits they had achieved for their employers. Rock 'n' roll had been introduced partially as a method to phase out these very malcontents. Drug use and hard living had been romanticized and even sometimes made mandatory for both jazz and rock musicians in order to keep the worker powerless and close to death, but with the expansion of the market translating into big profits and legal representation for musicians, more drastic changes had to be enacted.

Punk was a declaration of war against the virtuosos of rock and the synthesized beats of disco. Its creed was "poetry for everyone," that "anyone can do it," so it further defrocked the craftsmen of established genres. Its pretense was authenticity versus the plasticity of the status quo, which translated into a mythology of hard drugs, hard living, and identifying with poverty. The quest for fame was inverted, whereby something was less valuable by virtue of its notoriety, creating a lose-lose situation. The audience was transformed from consumers into competitors, whose conceit was often that they could do just as well as the poseur onstage.

The punk label, a petit bourgeois home business run by the enthusiast, was the preferred mode for proliferation of this product: the fanzine, an analogous magazine, the organ for information. Punk would remain marginalized throughout its existence because its invention constituted not the demise of the star, but the threat of his execution. Rock 'n' roll, looking death in the face, shrank from its demands of autonomy and fair treatment. The nurturing of groups became less and less common, resulting in a disposable system of contrived puppets prevailing again in the eighties. Punk was still retained as a deterrent, liberally shifting sound and shape like its rock 'n' roll twin/nemesis. Its official function is the invocation of authenticity as extortion.

While the punk phenomenon echoed

developments in bourgeois marketeering through grassroots distribution campaigns such as Amway, it was never paradigmatic in the way that its progenitors hoped. Instead, its aesthetic triumph was felt in the liberalization of violent and sexual content and the institutionalized disregard for the integrity of the artist/worker.

Just as the musician-as-artist was used to eclipse the newly agitating painter cells in the twenties, punk was used to rein in rock 'n' roll's attempts at greater self-determination. Punk, which expressed an apocalyptic nihilism ("no future"), was the corporate response to newly poignant environmental concerns spurred by Three Mile Island, Love Canal, and so on. It was capitalism without pretense of social conscience—the ruling class's proxy mouthpiece for voicing a virulent hatred of its subjects.

While thrilling for the ruling class as expression of this class hatred, punk could not be allowed to prevail due to the glut in production that it represented. While rock 'n' roll had perfectly echoed the producer-consumer relationship of the market system, punk's dynamic was producer-producer.

This was appropriate since punk, as a threat to upstart tool rock 'n' roll, was in fact the mirror of the bourgeoisie's uncensored bitching in the boardrooms and private yachts about their upstart seventies peons (environmental and consumer groups).

XIII. HIP HOP

Hip hop was praised on appearance by the scribes of the elite for the downsizing that it represented. An offshoot of a form originating in Jamaica, hip hop was commercially revolutionary, allowing for the recycling of records and the renewal of publishing mechanicals from long-forgotten songs.

Despite hip hop's derivative origins, it soon established itself as a futurist musical medium, disregarding rock 'n' roll's overwrought displays of instrument playing and virtuosity. The hip hop star was a personality with no particular craft except his ability to rap, a stance which built on punk's disavowal of musical scholarship. This rapper was a person who essentially spoke about himself, his desires, and his needs: the veritable personification of heroic capitalist individualism.

XIV. THE DJ

With American industry exported to impoverished slave states (Mexico, Taiwan, etc.), musicians no longer mirror their masters. The ruling class in the US no longer produces, but merely moves money through stocks and speculation; they are the designators of worth. The DJ is their star.

A preposterous poseur, once an adjunct to wedding parties, he is now exalted, featured in advertisements, and lavished with wealth and fame. He has become ubiquitous; no event is complete without one of these ninjas "spinning" their records.

Like the rulers on Wall Street, he has no actual talent except to play with other people's labor. His talent is his impeccable taste and his ability to turn junk into gold, like his stock-broking masters. His "scratching" of records is his display of contempt for the labor of his subjects.

The exaltation of the DJ is the ruling class congratulating itself for its good judgment in being born wealthy and in control of the world economy.

18

YOU CAN'T ALWAYS
GET NO SATISFACTION

In the winter of 2004, as CNN televised footage of schoolchildren being butchered in Russia by Chechen nationalists, the US's ruling class looked on jealously.

For fifty years, they had painstakingly perfected weapons designed expressly to kill those very children! As the Russians pulverized Chechnya in an orgy of vengeance and mass murder, this feeling of envy grew even more unbearable.

The Yankees had pioneered nerve gas, atomic bombs, hydrogen bombs, neutron bombs, intercontinental missiles, nuclear subs, and so on: multifarious and imaginative ways to dissect the babies and children of Mother Russia, splay them in gore against the ground, splatter them skyward atomically, or reduce them to microdust with megatons of plutonium. They were the bold custodians of a future that resembled the prayers of a moist-browed apocalypticist.

While social theorists once held forth on the idea of the future as a place free of race hate, war, and inequality, American overlords tenaciously defended their dystopian dream of destruction. They fought to transform scientific and social gains into tools of horror and atrocity, which were expressly designed to kill Russians. And they mostly succeeded.

But, despite their ingenuity and inspired hard work, they were only allowed to use their best weapons in meaningless pantomime exercises.

All their careful plans, concocted lovingly over decades, this country's own science elite working in splendid conjunction with the escaped Nazi doctors in their employ, gone to waste.

Their victory speech was on hand, already written. Through invocation of the FOIA

(Freedom of Information Act), copies of this speech have been obtained by resourceful individuals, though particular names and passages in the version we obtained had been blacked out (presumably by government censors):

"Ahem ... first, I'd like to thank the sinister beneficiaries of 'Operation Paperclip,' the massive US/Vatican effort to save Nazi war criminals from Soviet captivity, for all their work in developing the rockets that succeeded in exterminating these Russian *untermensch* scum.

[*Applause.*]

[*Aside to individual*] "No, [*person's name*]—we didn't forget you ..."

[*Laughter.*]

"Second, I'd like to thank our European lackeys for their splendid pose as 'Euro-communists' ... As the 'good cop' in the global scenario, you really had everyone going with

that welfare state, 'benevolent capitalism' stuff."

[*Applause.*]

"You should have heard all the
American college students, talking
about how great things are over
there!"

[*Applause and laughter.*]

"Hahahaa! Thankfully, it can end
now. Finally, and most of all, I'd like
to thank the American people for
their naivete in believing that Russia, a third world nation thousands
of miles away, with a GNP smaller
than Denmark's, was a threat to
them. Without their stupidity, com-
placency, and cosmic paranoia, we
could never have done it!"

[*Applause.*]

"But yes! Where others failed, we
have succeeded: the Red Beasts are
dead!"

[*Prolonged applause.*]

"This really pleases the Great Fly.

Slavs, with their susceptibility to alcohol, their abstract minds, and their emotional instability ... their genetic filthiness appointed them as the grand conquest of our superspecies ..."

The papers obtained through the FOIA also regale us with the details of a proposed dinner gala where this address was to be presented. According to the documents, the banquet they had appointed for the address was rather sumptuous. Though this banquet never ended up occurring (in the absence, thus far, of a Russia-exterminating nuclear holocaust), it had been planned out meticulously in advance. Like a nation's contingency plans for invading a neighbor, or the stockpiled obituaries of famous people at a newspaper, some projected future events are just too delightful to merely imagine and leave to the last moment. Though the affair was to be regal, it was actually only slightly more extravagant than the elite's usual soirees. From the papers we received, it seems that you can imagine these pretty well if you just squint your eyes, clench your jaw, and think about a Hammer horror film. If this is done correctly, it should evoke stardust memories of dream-factory scenarios of ritual dinners for well-to-do cabals.

While those are basically accurate depictions, the staged versions are actually a bit classier than the real thing, as Hollywood "punches up" the baby-eating ritual with an "old money" Euro-aristo veneer. The queen of England wouldn't be shown eating her buffalo wings with ketchup, for example, though that is her preference. And it wouldn't be revealed that the archbishop of Reims (yes, *that* archbishop of Reims) wears his robe to the table. Or that former Secretary of State James Baker is so preoccupied with fantasy football he can hardly be bothered to recite his portion of Doors lyrics during the nightly "Kronos ritual."

Still, despite the unfortunate vulgarity of the ruling elite, no cost is spared: Wolfgang Puck is often hired for the desserts, a top group like J. Geils Band might play, and Domino's provides all the pizza one could ever want, with toppings of every imaginable variety. After the sorbet, male, female, and transgender interns ply the banquet table, attending to the sensual needs of the powerful and potent. These naughty endeavors are sometimes adjourned early if *MacNeil/Lehrer* is on, or if the History Channel is showing a good special such as "Siege Weapons of the Middle Ages."

Such retreats, usually held in Sardinia, Connecticut, Stockholm, or Lyon, are not without their drama. Sometimes a CIA liaison bursts into a closed-door meeting to reveal something he has learned that day, whilst reading *Tintin*. When Alcazar was shown to be leading the Picaros against General Tapioca, for example, US bombers were immediately dispatched for the proper carnal sacrifice.

That type of state-subsidized ritual mass murder is a miniature version of the Western elite's projected genocide of Russians. Killing Russians as *untermensch* was based on the kind of eugenic philosophy expoed in *Dracula*, but also on the construction, in the capitalist countries, of the idea of the communists themselves as a *race group*. Because capitalism is a covert ideology that pretends that money relationships are completely natural, and that class doesn't exist, the communist must be despised in terms familiar to the normal discourse, either as a woman or as a racial-minority "other" type character. Therefore, the Commie was a "Red" or "pinko." In the wake of the Native American genocide, this new "fourth race" came about, modeled after the other "Red" victims of white conquest. Since the expansion of the US and Russian empires happened almost simultaneously as mirrors of one another (the Americans going west, as Muscovy went east), Russia was the US's inevitable "evil twin" nemesis (as Tocqueville predicted), its people replacing the subhuman natives as the white supremacist capitalist's ultimate prey (particularly after they went "Red"). This nascent confrontation preceded the official "Cold War." Hitler actually modeled his Russian-killing invasion tactics on the Indian-fighting exploits of his boyhood heroes from the books of German author Karl May.

Just as Judaism, under eugenics, ceased to be a religion and became first and foremost a race type (despite conversion to Judaism by gentiles through the ages), the communist was likewise no longer an ideologue with a particular critique of capitalism, but actually a despised kind of species of animal: *racially impure.* He had strange hair and smelled bad and wore no socks and underwear (as in Billy Wilder's *One, Two, Three*)—much like his Jewish consort, who was described in eugenics tracts as filthy and "ratlike." This caricature was jammed into the bourgeoisie's race ideology along with the rest of their jumbled esoterica. Hence the sexually hysteric overtones of the McCarthy "Red Scare" witch hunt, the mass murder of party members in concentration camps, and the slavish, fanatic denouncement of communism by the so-called liberal left, even in the age after communism. The melding of these race types—Jew, Slav, and Red—in the "Jewish-Bolshevik" archetype, provided a perfect storm for ritual slaying in the minds of the Western elite banking class. And a nuclear storm was the easiest, quickest funeral pyre, thought to please the commerce deity most, because of its playful "magic mushroom" design.

Alas, it was not to be so simple.

The Western rulers could simply never reconcile the radiation of gas and mineral resources with their desire for genocide of Russians. They loved money just slightly more than the giddily anticipated bath of blood. When they destroyed Chernobyl it was seen as an acceptable loss of (speculative) capital, leading as it did to the prostration of the socialist state; if the Slavs could not all be killed, they could at least be degraded.

This attrition strategy was Kennan's "great triumph": the arms race, the CIA sabotage of the Soviet's natural gas project in the eighties, and similar such operations eventually succeeded in bankrupting the USSR, and to its assets being procured by criminals and foreigners.

This fate was avoidable but actualized by

capitalist mole Gorbachev, who surrendered his country to "investors" and prompted a massive fire sale of state resources, a move commandeered by banking moguls and hailed as "market reform." The CIA helped install a government in its own image, called "the Mafia," and Russia sank into a quagmire of gangsterism.

As poverty and crime soared, American public intellectuals shook their heads in paternal condescension, pitying the poor dumb Russians for their naivete in embracing capitalism so fully and so quickly. Blaming the victims, they meanwhile pillaged the nation's final asset, its people, and the women of Russia were shipped off as sexual accessories to various imperial outposts, CIA fronts, and tax shelters, such as Israel, Bosnia, and Dubai. Still, though, it was an anticlimax. This daring American victory resulted in poverty and despair but not the fondly imagined carnage of a nuclear apocalypse.

And, as Smokey Robinson once said, sometimes "a taste of honey's worse than none at all."

During the Cold War, in lieu of the real thing, they had indulged their imaginations. As a spectacular replacement, directors like John Milius had dramatized the wonderful world of Slav slaughter in celluloid fantasies like *Red Dawn*. In these films, the Russian died differently than his German predecessor, going to his atheistic doom with materialist resignation, not unlike a worm after a rainstorm. Meanwhile, for the middle-class Anglophile, there were the adventures of secret agent James Bond, who always bedded his stunning SMERSH agent enemy before he killed her off. In this recurring Bond scenario, she wills her awful fate: after being mesmerized by his polymorphously perverse English public school penis, she could never go back to the bureaucratic touch of the apparatchik's methodical member.

Though these films and others like them served as a pleasant diversion, the rulers never got their imagined atomic blood sacrifice to their various Luciferic idols of commerce. And how their fingers had itched to push the button . . .

The proposed eruptions of Russian children's entrails often lured their hands momentarily from inside their trousers and toward the SAC code book. Over the red phone they would begin to mumble the nuke-code incantation, just as they'd whispered night after night in delirious half sleep … The silos would grind open, the jets would lift off—being careful to stay on course … steady … steady, and then—the bombardiers would launch their deadly load!

Then, in a moment of unusual sobriety, they would imagine the Soviet missile response, the resulting havoc it would wreak on their assets, the shrinking of their engorged bank accounts, and they would stay their hand in knightly discipline.

Attrition was the only answer. Even so, such business was boring and these masters of the universe were men—dashing and strong financiers, tennis bums, money launderers, and market manipulators, sprung from Ayn Rand's brow—and they had manly desires: to kill!

As proxies, the rulers armed Muslim tribes in Afghanistan to murder young Russian men and women. For the ruling class, these kinds of third-person conflicts are exciting gamesmanship, sort of like the "cockfighting" contests popular in the Southern United States. Sometimes the elites fund both sides, as in a number of African wars, so as to maximize the bloodshed for their insatiable owl-god.

Nearly 100,000 Afghans were paid and trained in a CIA-directed billion-dollar "jihad" fighting the Soviet army, a conflict which became an endless civil war. This was the US carryover of the very similar racist English pastime of the nineteenth century called the "Great Game." Designed to destabilize the Russian Empire through its "soft underbelly," the Englishmen who played the "Great Game" armed and fomented ethnic groups in that empire's diverse southern reaches. This "underbelly" included the Chechnya province of what is now the Russian Republic, Moscow's final foothold on the resource-rich region of the Caspian Sea.

The US has occupied the other southern reaches of the former USSR and turned them into armed camps and oil outposts for future exploitation.

There is little there to exploit now, but the important thing, when one is exploiting people, is to think in the long term. One must assess the situation at hand and think about any possibility that might arise in the future whereby one could exploit the situation. And if there seems even a small possibility of such future exploitation, one must place an army base there and buy or assassinate the political leaders of said place.

In the mid-1990s, Young Republican clubs in high schools across the Midwestern United States of America decided that Americans (North Americans) must no longer be so effeminate. Inspired by this decision, US government foreign policy is expressly designed to weaken any power that begins to compete with its primacy as explicated by the PNAC (Project for a New American Century), the "blueprint for maintaining global US preeminence, precluding the rise of a great power rival, and shaping the international security order in line with American principles and interests." In lieu of the impending energy crisis, the US has a strong interest in expelling Russia's final Caspian outpost along with their claims to that sea's oil and fish.

The Chechen guerrillas are the tools of choice, hapless pawns in the US/NATO geopolitical game, not dissimilar to the mujahideen or the "KLA" mafia who were so successfully designed to wreck Yugoslavia and its stubbornly socialist character.

The slaughter of children in southern Russia is merely another serial murder of Russians by the extraordinary Western ruling class. These pustulant vampires will run the live feed of the Beslan massacre from Russian TV, play it again and again at their ceremonies, until it pervades their dreams and becomes intertwined with their usual obscene sleepscape. But still for them it is not enough.

They want to be the ones to press the button, to pull the trigger, to rend the flesh: not just be the spook behind the wide-boy behind the greaseball behind the bagman at the snowy drop-off. They want to leave the skybox: to feel the Astroturf.

They're tired of writing checks!

At their metaphysical brunch, these ghouls sing with the bittersweet, tuneless pathos of the blood-drenched, drunken satanist, as they buckle up after another mechanistic, overlit sex-magick ritual.

"I can't always get no satisfaction," they whine as they watch the horror.

"But you might find . . ." comfort in the knowledge that they have destroyed all organized resistance to their numeric ideology; that now they are kings of all they survey just for some abstract figure on a bank slip.

". . . you get what you need."

They raise their glass of vodka: "Skoal."

PERSONAL INSCRIPTION

Dear _____ ,

I know. An explanation is in order. You must attempt to understand. I will delineate using numbers to help clarify.

1. Electronic impulses have been transmitted to us, a few at a time and over a period. They have compelled us to inscribe the meditations contained in this volume.

2. These impulses are revealed as *The Psychic Soviet*.

3. It reveals itself cunningly: a flickering aura around the obfuscations by the satanic bedbugs of officiation, spurring those attuned to become "mystics of action."

4. We, too, have questions. Is it a force which begs a physical manifestation? Is it a vagabond cosmonaut, trapped in space, helplessly witnessing events on earth? The final, isolated ideologue? Are we its chosen expression? Are we its weapon?

5. It reassures us through the sentiments it transmits that it—though hoary specter or astral manta—is firmly rooted in materialism.

6. Behind its bilious exegesis, it desires transformation alongside the apocalyptic extermination of its foes, seeing the two ambitions as inseparable.

7. It leads our hand as it writes and we follow its encrypted path willingly, fanatically . . . a lover enraptured.

8. We are enchanted by the cruelty of its conceits and the brilliant truth it reveals.

9. Despite social consternation, we recognize the *Soviet* for what it is: the final bulwark against collective hypnosis by our arch enemy, the *Knights of Ordo Novus Etcetera*.

10. Its ordinations are dangerous: incendiary, flung like Greek fire over the ramparts at the seething mass of brain controllers and amoralist nincompoops who comprise the apologist functionaries of our imperial culture.

11. Still, it is piss in the ocean.

12. Their attack continues: interminable, unabated.

13. Through all their various conduits, the enemies unveil their bizarre master plan via dictums regarding beauty, worth, morality, the meaning of history, and the political implications of the select "world events" we are privy to.

14. These international happenings, stage-managed theater events, are designed by occult psychologists to trigger particular primitive reactions and impulses in a global audience they view as so much warm meat.

15. Not only so-called politics are packaged for us. The history of "culture" receives particular scrutiny from establishment revisionists, intent on controlling the meaning of the products, events, and phenomena of aesthetic endeavor.

16. A fantasy narrative is assembled from which the ruling class suspends our consciousness and from which we select our "lifestyle choices": the pathetic shell game which we daily engage as eternal marks.

17. One must summon a defense system, a cerebral citadel, a *Psychic Soviet*, to protect oneself against this ulterior attack.

18. In between our momentary lapses of consciousness, we must cloister ourselves in this final rampart.

19. Using this system, we have waged a gory campaign on the precepts of "art," "rock 'n' roll," "performance," and the official ideas of their function in the culture.

20. For this struggle, we are despised offhandedly by the masters and savagely by their house servants, those average cretins who wish to maintain their unexamined barony of decontextualized self-reference.

21. They have responded with all the pesticides in their arsenal: intimidation, ridicule, sexual resentment, indifference, physical harm, and poverty.

22. They seethe against the valor of our aggregates; our appearance reveals that they, wrapped with inane puerility and cosmic

vacuity, are mere running-dog lackeys for the overlords.

23. The physical and critical forces they have arrayed against us are awesome; they use all their strength to destroy us.

24. Still, there is never surrender.

25. This degradation has been survived only through channeling *The Psychic Soviet*, which armors us against our enemies' relentless, insidious offense.

26. Though the culture maintains an institutionalized disregard for the meaning and impact of so-called art, the CIA station in Hollywood and the massive federal subsidization of American film, painting, and music reveal the ruling class's tacit recognition of its enormous ideological power, both as export and as agent for domestic control.

27. Deviant strains of these art forms are starved and confounded to an asymmetrically profound extent.

28. In the two-dimensional arena—the world where words sit on paper—rock 'n' roll's attempts at autonomy and metamorphosis have been annihilated.

29. The reactionary proclamations of official revisionists have determined an official version of cultural history, though this changes per their needs.

30. These arbiters determine the content of supposedly market-driven popular art forms through aesthetic pronouncements and control of history, proliferated massively through all media outlets.

31. Through these totems, the subjects are taught to glean values and behavioral modes, as well as lessons regarding relations between sex, "race," age, and class.

32. As with other wars, the package is marketed by the usual Madison Avenue krewe.

33. Their empire, the popular consciousness, was successfully conquered long ago and is now their exclusive domain, reserved for their rampant molestation.

34. Their arrogance has expanded as their prey becomes more passive.

35. The baldness of intent which characterizes recent conquest only illuminates the degree to which they feel unchallenged, omnipotent.

36. And for good reason.

37. Their one, final enemy is the *Soviet* and the specter of cynical instinct upon which the outrageous conceits of this book are based.

38. That this grain of improbability should

impress itself into their waistbands as their nemesis is our fervent wish; that it should foster discomfort, infection, and convulsive rejection of the impoverished story line we inherit.

39. These essays, though apparently demolishing one another in contradictory eruptions, attempt to subvert the official narrative and shine a light on its fantastical intent, simultaneously empowering those multitudes who have been brushed aside for their threatening ideological clarity.

40. Therefore, *The Psychic Soviet*—

41. (personal message).

42. SMERT SPIONEM!

43. Yours,_____

AFTERWORD

Notes on The Psychic Soviet
for the Second Edition

When *The Psychic Soviet* first appeared, it was described in reviews as "extravagant," "awry," "delusional," and "dangerous."

Those who scanned it were scandalized. Those who read it were reddened. Its discontents were legion.

Whether it was an ivory tower academic, who saw the book as a harbinger of their coming irrelevance, or a retired billionaire, wary of a new front in the class war, the book was regarded with fear and anxiety. Book publishers were threatened by its outsider model, while armchair rock theorists were jealous of its scope and daring. Whether they were foreign dignitaries, minor league mafiosi, or presidents of private sex clubs, nearly everyone who cracked open *The Psychic Soviet* was aghast that it might upset their personal apple cart. It was banned from university curriculums, summer reading groups, and from being recited aloud at the United Nations. Organizers of art bookfairs conspired to crush it underfoot. Librarians were encouraged to file it under the "insane" or "gibberish" section at the bibliotheque. As there was no precedent for this kind of book, the Dewey decimal system was unable to accommodate it.

Since *The Psychic Soviet*'s findings were incendiary, the book was predictably suppressed, and a copy was difficult—nearly impossible—to find. Of course one might locate one; perhaps in the pocket of a gin-soaked tramp, ruthlessly rolled by ruffians—or maybe on the body of a waterlogged spy, washed up dead on a remote shore—but the instances of its appearance were unusual and rare.

Still, thrill seekers sought it out, as intently as a narcotic enthusiast scours the street for a new pill or powder that's rumored to be fatal. The few copies in existence passed feverishly from paw to paw, as old ideas of ownership were forgotten, traded in for egalitarianism and idea sharing; *The Psychic Soviet*'s acolytes understood the book signaled new possibilities, new values.

The social planners who organize society understood as well. Catastrophe struck the literary world, as stores were run out of business, shuttered, shut down, and demolished. Bookshops—once cultural hubs of any self-respecting population center—suddenly became scarce, rarefied.

This diabolical transformation of the landscape is typically credited to the electronic mail-order innovation called "the Internet," which led to the dust bowl desolation dubbed "gentrification." But some whisper that *The Psychic Soviet* was responsible. Indeed, certain sinister forces were avowed in their determination that the book not proliferate. Wrecking the institutions where words were sold would be the most effective manner to do so.

Bookstores weren't just bulldozed outright, of course; they were made obsolete via a profound and insidious transformation of humankind's relationship to the written word. This was done through an acceleration of the postwar newspeak called "Branding," which developed from the consumer culture that had replaced ideological systems intended to create a less exploitative, more humane world.

A brand is a jumble of letters or words written in a distinct style, typically designating a particular make of a product. These letters, words, or numbers insinuate, if not the superiority of the owner, a firm perch for them in a universe otherwise hewn from chaos. These logos alleviate anxiety for the holder of the brand, and induce anxiety in those without. Brands were obviously not a new concept, but in the post-Soviet era, with the population shorn of idealism, humanism, hope for the future, and any ideology aside from consumerism, people turned to product names and logos as a dogma. The brand names became a sort of Esperanto; a pan-global pidgin that promulgated particular values and proliferated the aesthetic of consumption both as catharsis and creed.

The "Brandish" that people began to speak had profound implications. Once, letters, alphabets, and words had been tools for conveying ideas, concepts, and desires. But with logos imbued with sacred value, words and letters became glyphs: abstract and symbolic.

A new emphasis on branding in the post-Soviet universe was, for global social planners, the key to changing a population's relationship not only to competing ideologies—those at odds with the capitalist planners' own creed of racism, iniquity, exploitation, etc.—but to letters and words themselves, transforming them from tools into totems. The users of such an alphabet would be reduced to something more compliant and less unruly; like barnyard animals. Artists, being the first "brands" (starting with Michelangelo, da Vinci, et al.), were the rehabilitators par excellence of Brandish to the middle classes.

Just as the Romantic artists—confronted by the wreckage wrought by the Industrial Revolution—painted ancient forests which were quickly being eradicated by new, soot-belching factories, so the artists of today prefer to paint a big word, a letter or two, or a sentence fragment on a canvas, as they sense the imminent demise of language itself.

In such a landscape, where any word or set of initials is imbued with mysticism, part of a magical pantheon, the coherent sentence suddenly seems garish, baroque, overwrought, and absurd. And a book seems ridiculous. This sensibility precipitated the rampant, pitiless immolation of the bookstore, and transpired via mind controllers from Madison Avenue who were in turn inspired, some would say, by *The Psychic Soviet*.

To make things even more complicated for *The Psychic Soviet,* the book field was soiled by an influx of lookalike decoy "art" books from vanity presses, almost indistinct from *The Psychic Soviet* aside from their vacancy and pointlessness. But their form was practically identical.

After *The Psychic Soviet*, these books muddied the landscape with nonsense, and *The Psychic Soviet'*s message was often confused with these little tomes.

Now, in a postsentence landscape, where a book is a series of pages stapled together to display girth and volume instead of content, *The Psychic Soviet*'s new volume seems an outlier. Its as ferocious as ever, more relevant, uncannily prescient, and made more sophisticated from its exile. What possible use could this kind of book be in a universe where the only goal is acquisition of a chrome cashmere top paired with mesh-webbing undergarments? This volume, like the last, has been outfitted with a series of subversive logos, featured on the pages preceding each chapter, which will infiltrate the consciousness of the brand-soaked modern, and which will steer citizens toward radical action and insurrection. This is the promise of *The Psychic Soviet, Mk II*.

Sincerely,
Ian F. Svenonius
Author

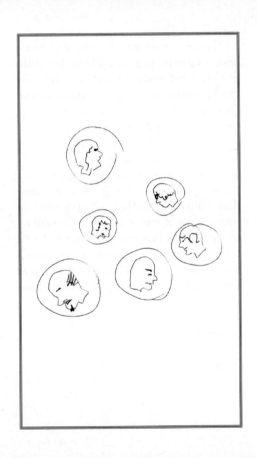

THE PSYCHICK PSKETCHBOOK

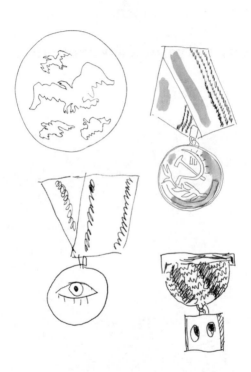

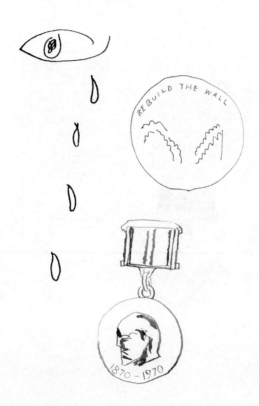

REBUILD THE WALL

1870 - 1970

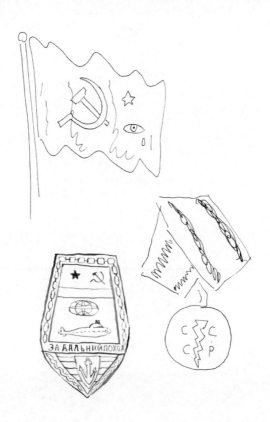

Notes

Notes

Notes

Notes

Notes